Hire Smart and Keep 'Em

Hire Smart and Keep 'Em

How to Interview Strategically Using POINT

Joan C. Curtis

Foreword by Patsy Hammett

 PRAEGER

AN IMPRINT OF ABC-CLIO, LLC
Santa Barbara, California • Denver, Colorado • Oxford, England

Library of Congress Cataloging-in-Publication Data

Curtis, Joan C., 1950–
  Hire smart and keep 'em : how to interview strategically using POINT / Joan C. Curtis ; foreword by Patsy Hammett.
    p. cm.
  Includes bibliographical references and index.
  ISBN 978–1–4408–0286–7 (hard copy : alk. paper) — ISBN 978–1–4408–0287–4 (ebook)
1. Employment interviewing. I. Title.
HF5549.5.I6C865 2012
658.3'1124—dc23   2012010982

ISBN: 978–1–4408–0286–7
EISBN: 978–1–4408–0287–4

16 15 14 13 12   1 2 3 4 5

This book is also available on the World Wide Web as an eBook.
Visit www.abc-clio.com for details.

Praeger
An Imprint of ABC-CLIO, LLC

ABC-CLIO, LLC
130 Cremona Drive, P.O. Box 1911
Santa Barbara, California 93116-1911

This book is printed on acid-free paper ∞

Manufactured in the United States of America

I am not afraid of storms, for I am learning how to sail my ship.

—Louisa May Alcott

I dedicate this book to my amazing mom, who taught me the value of learning and who continues to live as if each day were a new ship to sail.

Contents

Foreword

How to recruit and retain the best talent is on the mind of human resource executives every day because it is on the mind of their organizations' chief leaders. In today's world, there really is a war for talent. Top talent wants to work for top organizations. Top organizations must brand themselves as employers of choice. In the end, company executives must attract, select, and hire the best and the brightest for their organizations. This is what makes a top organization. Jim Collins made this clear in his bestselling book, *Good to Great*. He wrote that great companies get the right people on the bus.

Having led the recruiting process for a global manufacturing company for almost 18 years, I can say firsthand that recruiting top talent today is more difficult and challenging than ever. Technology has changed the playing field in terms of how we source candidates, communicate with candidates, and even interview candidates. With the impact of technology, we now have more reason than ever to be focused on the "high touch" of recruiting. Connecting with candidates before, during, and after interviews is a critical part of the formula for hiring the best and the brightest.

If you want to be successful in hiring top talent, Joan's book *Hire Smart and Keep 'Em: How to Interview Strategically Using POINT* will help you. I know because not only have I learned and used her strategic interviewing approach and her POINT system, but I have also made this training available to hundreds of recruiters at the company for which I work.

Joan understands how to create a successful and effective interview process that includes keeping the interview legal. This is a must in today's world. Companies strive to conduct business in an ethical manner. Without this knowledge, managers stand to put themselves and their organizations in ɔpardy. In today's competitive environment, companies cannot afford to ɹave a negative brand resulting from illegal questions during an interview.

Beyond this basic, managers need to understand that effective interviewing is not an innate skill, as too many individuals believe. As this book demonstrates, effective interviewing involves multiple, complex skills that work together to get you the right hire. Joan's POINT system addresses the key essentials—from the job description, to planning and preparing for the interview, to creating the right behavior-based questions specifically targeted to the individual, to creating an open environment for a successful interview, and finally to fine-tuning highly focused listening skills. The following pages also provide you with the exceptionally valuable ability to assess yourself as an interviewer. With this unique component, you can continue to improve as an interviewer.

Effective interviewers whose knowledge, skills, and performance bring top talent to their organization are tremendously valued and respected. This book will teach you how to become one of those valued and respected people.

Patsy Hammett
Corporate Recruiting Manager, Milliken & Company
www.milliken.com

Introduction

Managers get things done through others. Can you accomplish that task without hiring smart? Martin Yate in *Hiring the Best* says, "No one knows how many managers have stalled their careers through an inability to make the right hires."[1] Yet throughout my career as an instructor, coach, and consultant, I hear managers say, "Interviewing is not really my job. I'm an engineer (or I'm an accountant or I'm a whatever)." Too often managers rely on human resource personnel to conduct the interviews. When they see candidates, they think they can get away with just "visiting." This is one reason companies waste billions of dollars on hiring mistakes. Hiring goes beyond human resource managers. They can screen candidates for you, but the actual selection falls on the manager. If you consider interviewing as a secondary part of your job, you are in grave trouble. Mornell, in his book *Hiring Smart: How to Predict Winners and Losers*, suggests that the cost of hiring mistakes is at a minimum one-and-one-half times the person's annual salary.[2] He says *at a minimum* because he presumes the mistake will be rectified in six months. If it is not, the costs escalate.

As a manager, you can't afford to make mistakes if you want to hire smart and keep those people you eventually chose.

WHY READ THIS BOOK

Imagine this scenario: You spend time writing a job description. You pull together a team of people to help you isolate job competencies. Then you pour money into placing the job listing in appropriate trade journals. You visit sites where candidates work or study. You might even hire a headhunter to

ـou find the best people to interview. Once you find a pool of people, you ـn through the hundreds of résumés and applications that come across ـr desk. In this tight job market, you can expect five times more applicaـns than you received just a few years ago. You devote hours to culling ـut the best people to talk to. That accomplished, you assign a team of people to talk to the final two to four candidates. You put up money to fly in the candidates and house them in a nearby hotel. You and others take them to dinner the night before the interview. The next day is devoted to interviewing—you and several of your staff spend time talking to the candidate, taking her on tours, listening to her presentation. The day is basically shot. The same thing happens for each candidate. After completing the interviews, you and your team decide on the best candidate. Finally you make an offer.

The person arrives on the first day of work. As soon as the newbie begins, you realize you've made a huge hiring mistake. All that work has been for nothing and must begin again. This person will not suit. No wonder managers are frustrated.

Some managers decide to keep the bad employee simply because they don't want to go through the entire process again. It's too costly. They rationalize that the employee just needs a bit more time, a bit more support. The person stays, and other employees get frustrated, wondering why management hasn't gotten rid of this incompetent person. Soon your team gives up and begins to look elsewhere for work. You start to lose your best talent.

You've expended time, money, and resources. The company devoted endless capital to making sure the hiring process went well. How could everyone make such a mistake? What went wrong?

Unfortunately, what went wrong in this scenario goes wrong in offices throughout the country every day. *Managers know how to recruit, but they don't know how to interview. To hire smart, managers must do both.*

The purpose of this book, *Hire Smart and Keep 'Em: How to Strategically Interview Using POINT*, is to show managers *how to interview the right way.* When the door closes and you are sitting across from that candidate, what happens next? What skills do you need to make sure you uncover the truth behind the candidate's smile? How can you probe candidates until they tell you something they didn't intend to tell you? How can you hire someone who can do the job and not someone who simply knows how to interview?

Strategic interviewers using POINT practice the skills necessary to hire smart. This book will show you those skills. It will not provide a quick and dirty formula (as many books out there claim to do). It will illustrate the complexities of interviewing. Interviewing effectively takes skill and practice. *You cannot hope to hire smart and hire easy.* Just like with anything of value, you have to work to get it right.

Strategic interviewing is an advanced method of *listening and questioning* designed to strip away the superficial to get at the truth about a candidate's

ability to perform the key tasks needed to do a job. The POINT proc
step-by-step approach to strategic interviewing.[3] I coined the term in m
book, *Strategic Interviewing: Skills and Tactics for Savvy Executives.*
What can you expect from reading this book?

1. A clear understanding of what strategic interviewing is and how other
   kinds of interviews, structural and laissez faire, fail in their attempts
   to strip away the superficial.

2. An overview of how to write job descriptions, conduct virtual interviews, and set up a professional recruiting process, including tips for
   recruiting in online communities.

3. Examples of how communication and listening skills play a vital role in
   the interview itself. A clear understanding of behavior-based interviewing and how to create questions that are based on a person's past.

4. A healthy respect for the role of trust in the interview environment,
   with examples of ways the interviewer can establish trust by being open
   and using strategic icebreakers.

5. A step-by-step description of the POINT process to help discover the
   value of putting the interview at the center of any recruiting operation.
   Skill and practice in the six intentional listening skills: probe, paraphrase, summary, reality test, flipside, and reflection.

6. Guidelines for interviewing without breaking the law.

7. Tips for team interviewing and the skills necessary for conducting
   interviews with a partner.

8. Practice exercises to help you appraise your own listening and communication skills in the interview environment.

HIRE SMART AND KEEP 'EM

In this book we will give you examples and exercises to show you how to
conduct a strategic interview using the POINT process. When you apply the
system outlined in these pages, you will increase your chances of hiring smart
and making sure those people you hire stay. The key is to take the mystery out
of interviewing. We will open the interview up and reveal its underbelly. You
will see the things that work and the things that don't work. You'll experience
through real interview examples what goes on behind that closed door.

At the end of 10 chapters, you'll find exercises, cases, or assessments. If
you work through these exercises, you will sharpen your ability to hire smart.

Remember, to hire smart, you must hire strategically. Each candidate
brings to the table different knowledge, skills, and experiences. If you ask

questions of every person, you are not interviewing strategically. ard managers say, "I ask the same question to every candidate to see neir responses vary." What's the point of that? How can seeing varied onses strip away the superficial to get at the real person? Your goal is . to trick candidates but *to create a safe environment that encourages them to tell you something they had not intended to say.* In the planning phase of POINT the individualized, strategic interview plan takes shape. Managers identify target competencies and create suitable questions to probe those points. These questions vary from one candidate to the next.

One skill you will learn in POINT is how to dig deeper by piggy-backing questions. Rather than taking the interview in a totally different direction, you will learn the importance of piggy-backing to learn more and more. During my workshops I've watched countless interviews where each question the interviewer asks has nothing to do with the candidate's response. One time I stopped an interview right after the candidate spoke and asked the interviewer, "What did the candidate just say?" That interviewer didn't have a clue. No wonder we make hiring mistakes.

THE POINT PROCESS

The POINT process is a step-by-step approach to strategic interviewing. POINT takes the interview from the beginning to the end, with the heart of the process being the middle: *the actual interview.*

The *P* in POINT stands for *Plan.* It represents everything from the recruitment of appropriate candidates to the planning before the actual interview itself. Planning includes résumé screening, writing job descriptions, isolating competencies, and checking references. It also includes organizing the actual day of interviews. Planning means identifying what you will ask each candidate. Once you isolate your competencies, you compare those with the résumé. If, for example, you have a candidate that clearly demonstrates a competency you are searching for, there's no need to spend time probing that area further. This doesn't mean you believe everything on the résumé. You check it out, but not with the same intensity.

The *O* in POINT stands for *Open.* You cannot hope to strip away the superficial unless you create trust. The strategic interview uses intentional listening as a way to build trust and a sense of openness. Think about your own situations in which you've experienced trust. Were you across the desk, facing a potential employer? Probably not. The challenge of the interviewer is to turn the interview into a place of trust. This is the hardest job of the interview. Openness also means interviewing deeper than the superficial. *To strategically interview, you probe the entire person—not simply that person's work persona.* How would you like to hire a mass murderer who happens to be

INTENTIONAL LISTENING SKILLS DEFINED

Probe	An open question that seeks to find out more information about something.
Paraphrase	A statement that rephrases in your words what the person just said it; has an understood question mark at the end.
Flipside	A probe that forces the person to share an opposite side.
Reality Test	A series of probes and paraphrases designed to test the reality of what was said.
Summary	A series of paraphrases that summarize what was said.
Reflection	A statement that requires you to reflect (as in a mirror) the feelings you hear behind the words being expressed.

great at information technology? Most managers dwell on specific skills and abilities and forget about interests and hobbies. When you look beyond the superficial, you must dig deeper. In this book you'll learn why openness is important and how to create an interview environment that fosters trust.

The *IN* in POINT stands for *intentional listening*. Listening with intent is the heart of the POINT process and strategic interviewing. Notice what this means. You not only listen with your full antenna alert, but you also listen for the competencies you have identified in the planning phase. You might ask a question about leadership, and the candidate tells you about a conflict situation. Conflict management might be one of your competencies. Your attention rises, and you probe conflict as well as leadership. *Intentional listening requires you to be on full alert throughout the interview*. You cannot allow your senses to relax. It requires the highest form of communication and listening.

The intentional listening skills that we will address in this book are the probe, paraphrase, summary, reality test, flipside, and reflection.

The *T* in POINT stands for *Test*. Once the interview is over, it's time to test its effectiveness. Many books talk about how to evaluate the candidate and how to test the recruiting process. These two components play a significant role in the interview testing process. Few books, however, talk about how to test the interview itself

Imagine a scenario where you attract a candidate with excellent credentials, incredible communications skills, and the highest references from previous

...periences. On the surface, he looks like a perfect fit for your job. You ...he candidate through a very professional recruiting system. Unfortu- ...y, your interviewers do not dig or strip away the superficial. They talk ...out themselves. Each one asks the same or similar questions. At the end ... the day you offer the candidate the job—after all, the person had great communication skills and wonderful references—even though you learned little more from the interviews than you knew from the résumé and referen- ces. The candidate comes to work. Once he arrives, the candidate realizes this job is not a good fit. He leaves within three months of the hire. Oops. Did you hire smart?

Testing the interview and its effectiveness is as important as testing the recruiting process and the candidate. This third prong will cause the best sys- tem to collapse if it is ignored.

Chapters 1 and 2 will define strategic interviewing and introduce the POINT process. You will understand the basic communication skills and the power of the nonverbal message. You'll read about all aspects of the preinter- view, including the recruitment process. You will learn the components of a good job description and how to establish clear competencies. These chapters will also address recruiting in the virtual world, including telephone inter- views and appropriate use of tools like Skype, Google Talk, or other technol- ogy for recruitment and preliminary screening, as well as the power of LinkedIn as a recruiting tool.

Chapters 3 and 4 will define behavior-based interviews and team inter- views. You'll see how a behavior-based focus enables the interviewer to strip away the superficial. Rather than spend time talking about a person's projec- tion of what she can do in the future, you will learn how to talk about what she's actually done in the past. Chapter 4 will introduce team interviews and give you tips for interviewing with a partner. The skills you need for team interviewing require even more strategic planning than a one-on-one inter- view. You'll see how to diminish the power of perception by interviewing in teams and how teams can increase the chances of hiring smart and keeping them.

Chapter 5 will give you a clear-cut view of all the legal issues surrounding interviews. You'll learn what not to ask. You'll also learn why interviews have become so legally sensitive and how the POINT process works to keep your interview legal.

Chapter 6 will look at opening the interview. You'll learn why trust and openness are important to strip away the superficial. You'll get a clear idea of how to balance questions related to work and outside interests. You will experience the power of the Johari window and see how trust and respect affect the interview while you learn how to create strategic icebreakers.

Chapter 7 through 9 will look at intentional listening in the POINT process. You'll understand how important it is to listen with intent and the skills

needed to do so. You'll have an opportunity to practice each of the skills
see them in action. You'll see which intentional listening skills play a
strongest role in interviews and which are less prominent. Timing and balance
are essential to effective use of intentional listening. You'll become a skilled
listener who pays attention when someone lets slip something he didn't intend
to say.

Chapter 10 will examine the testing part of POINT. You'll learn how to
evaluate yourself as an interviewer. Did you ask too many closed questions?
Did you piggy-back your questions? Were your questions legal? Did you
uncover something that you did not expect? In this section you'll have an
opportunity to evaluate other interviews for effectiveness using guides for testing the strategic interviewer and the strategic interviewing process.

Chapter 11 will examine sticky situations in interviews. Not all candidates
are professional. Not all candidates play by the rules. What do you do when
you encounter someone who tries to force your hand on something that may
be legally sensitive? How do you deal with a candidate who openly flirts with
you or asks you to do something that may be unethical? You'll learn how to
stay profrofessional when faced with these sorts of situations.

Chapter 12 will explore retention. Even though using the POINT process
will increase the likelihood that you will keep the people you hire, there are
other issues you need to consider. In Chapter 12 we'll look at those issues
to enable you to not only hire smart but also to retain those people you do
hire.

Finally, after you finish reading *Hire Smart and Keep 'Em*, you will be in
an ideal position to conduct your first strategic interview. This book will prepare you to tackle the challenge of hiring smart every time. It will give you
what you need to diminish hiring mistakes. It will equip you with the skills
to hire the right people on your team and thereby enable you to get the job
done. Basically, it will take the mystery out of interviewing and tell you
how to do it.

ONE

What Do You Know about Interviewing?

What does it take to pick the right person for the right job? What prompts you to make that all-important selection? The psychology of the interview process has mystified managers for generations. They've spent countless hours searching for clear-cut guidelines to help guide them through the murky waters.

To understand the complexity of interviewing, we must start at the beginning and look at a bit of history. Some managers see interviewing as an intuitive process that cannot be learned. "The biggest blind spot hiring managers have in our recruiting experience is that they believe that their 'intuition' will guide them to the correct hire. They look at a strict process as being 'cold,' time consuming, or just not worth the effort,"[1] wrote Dan Erling in *Match*. That kind of thinking has led to costly hiring mistakes and endless confusion about the interview. It's that kind of thinking that has led many managers to skip training and toss their new managers out there, saying, "Here's a candidate. Talk to him and if you like him, start him to work on Monday."

Indeed, most of us have had no training in interviewing, which, by the way, is one of the most important jobs you'll have as a manager. Lou Adler tells us in *Hire with Your Head* that when he landed his first job in a Fortune 100 company with no interview training, he was sent on a corporate recruiting trip. In other words he was a newly hired employee with no training in recruiting sent out to find people to hire for the entire company! The head of human resources gave him three minutes of interviewing advice.[2] You might think this example unusual, but unfortunately it represents the norm. *Your success in hiring can make or break your career.* Instead of beginning with the assumption that you know how to interview and what an interview is, let's assume you know nothing and start at the beginning.

...G THE INTERVIEW

...nard Olson defined interviewing as, "A set of verbal and ...verbal ...actions between two or more people focused on gathering i... ...mation ...decide a course of action."[3]

This definition tells you that your decision—to hire or not hire—...based on "a set of verbal and nonverbal interactions." If you are a manager, y...are probably thinking, "what does that mean?" Indeed, sets of verbal and no...erbal interactions are not clear; they are vague. Imagine telling your boss...ou want to hire someone because you liked her set of verbal and nonverbal ...teractions. What response might that evoke? Clearly, then, the decision to ...re someone is not based on sheer fact—whether he went to Harvard or has e...erience flying super jets. The decision to hire someone is based on much more...nd that much more is not something you can put your finger on. *This is our fir... clue that interviewing is not a straightforward process lending itself to a s...eadsheet and numbers. Instead, it is a challenge that must be faced with a h...althy dose of respect.*

The second thing you notice in the definition is the term *interaction*. What does interaction say to you? As a manager you k...ow that one of your biggest challenges is dealing with people. You may have lots of knowledge about the particular fields you are in, whether it's medicine, law, or academics, but when you add people to the mix, everything turns topsy-turvy. A fantastic surgeon who demands that people respond to his every need, disregarding what is best for the patient, leaves staff frustrated, angry, and polishing up their résumés. These kinds of problems—interactions among and between people—cause more trouble than anything else you face. *Interviewing is all about interaction—* interaction between the interviewer and the candidate and vice versa, as well as interaction among fellow interviewing colleagues.

The third important component of Olson's definition of interviewing is the insistence that you make a decision. With most other decisions in management, you can postpone your decision by spending time gathering more information or by asking others to look into the matter for you. But once you exit an interview, you must make a decision; time is of the essence. Thumbs up or thumbs down—should you hire or not? This puts tremendous pressure on the interviewer. Adler advises waiting before making a decision. He says time will help improve the selection success. Unfortunately, as most managers know, candidates don't wait. If you are not quick to decide, the good candidates disappear. Waiting alone will not guarantee success.

The final and most important aspect of Olson's definition is the concept of verbal and nonverbal interactions. Nonverbal interactions are sensations, not particular information you hear or see. *Putting nonverbal cues in the mix means the interview decision is not based on fact but on feeling.* How can a manager make a professional, clear-headed decision when the basis for that decision is feeling?

Looking at these four important pieces of the interview leads you critical question. *Is there a way to conduct an interview that will help ager hire smart and keep 'em and avoid the pitfalls of a subjective, i decision?* The answer to that question is yes. When managers interview stra cally using the POINT process, they increase the odds of hiring successfully

THE EVOLUTION OF THE STRATEGIC INTERVIEW

Again, given that most of us know little to nothing about interviewing even though we've been at it for years, let's begin with a little history. Back when businesses were small mom-and-pop operations, interviews were very informal. Someone who knew someone came to talk to you, and if you liked that person, you hired him or her. Hiring mistakes cost little. If you erred, you started over. New employees walked right in and did the job with little or no training. The process of interviewing did not exist. This kind of interview became known as the laissez-faire interview. Imagine the interviewer leaning back in her chair and talking to the candidate about herself and her experiences. In the laissez-faire interview the interviewer talked over 70 percent of the interview time. This interviewer's goal was to get to know the candidate informally. Jobs were not complex. A candidate's ability to do the job mattered little. Much of the interview decision was based on personality, emotions, biases, chemistry, and stereotypes, not on clear-cut competencies.

Laissez-faire interviewing dominated for a long time, well into the early part of the twentieth century, and some may argue it still exists today. The Industrial Age brought with it large businesses with bureaucracies where laissez-faire interviewing no longer worked. Bigger businesses recognized that they could not trust these informal interviews to produce quality hiring decisions. In response, the companies swung the pendulum in the opposite direction. What emerged was the structured interview.

When I began training interviewers over 15 years ago, structured interviewing was what companies wanted their managers to learn. Companies demanded consistency in interviewing. In other words, they wanted a structured set of questions that managers asked every candidate without regard to the candidate's particular skills or experiences. The other factor that came into play with the Industrial Age was litigation. When people began suing big business for the so-called biases characterizing the laissez-faire interview, companies looked for something entirely different. Furthermore, as interviewing penetrated deeper into the organization, owners (and CEOs) sought to maintain control. The more people interviewing, the greater the risk for lawsuits or costly hiring mistakes. The solution was a structured interview.

Both laissez-faire and structured interviewing have problems in today's world. These types of interviews represent polar opposites. The laissez-faire interview, characterized by too much freedom, tells you nothing about the

...d exposes managers to criticism or lawsuits. The structured inter-
...ne other hand, characterized by too much formality, shuts... listen-
...tells you nothing about the candidate. Both result in frustration... hiring
...es, leading managers to scratch their heads in frustration... can we
...e an interview process that allows for both informality... structure but
...eals important information about the candidate?

THE BIRTH OF STRATEGIC INTERVIEWING

There are some good things about the laissez-faire interview. For one, the interview is conversational. For another, the interview feels informal, and informality enables the candidate to relax. Those are good things. Unfortunately the focus of the laissez-faire interview is not on the candidate but on the employer and the job. The interviewer eats up 70 or more percent of the interview time. *Strategic interviewing shifts the focus from the employer to the candidate but keeps the informality and conversational feel.* One important component of a strategic interview is openness—hence, the O in the POINT process. Interviewers look for ways to enable the candidate to open up and share information he probably didn't intend to share when he walked in the door. Candidates do that when they feel as if they are having a relaxed conversation with someone they trust, not when they feel interrogated. As we'll see later in this book, *trust is one of the key ingredients of the strategic interview and one of the most difficult to accomplish.*

The structured interview, too, has some good aspects. It isn't haphazard; it has a purpose and a direction—it has parameters. Unfortunately, again the focus of the structured interview is not the candidate but the job. Regardless of the candidate and what she says, structural interviewers ask the same questions. Strategic interviewers, on the other hand, shift the focus to the candidate but keep the parameters. In a strategic interview every question has a purpose. Strategic interviewers resemble detectives sifting through a mass of clues for just the right one. They must filter through everything with dogged determination until that one significant piece of evidence surfaces.

Strategic interviewing takes the best of laissez-faire and structural interviewing and combines them into a new process that focuses on the candidate. *Strategic interviewing therefore is an interviewing process that focuses on a candidate's past behavior to strip away the superficial in order to discover what lies underneath.*

Let's analyze an example of a short interview and determine what kind of interview it represents:

Interviewer: I see you went to Rutgers University.
Candidate: Yes, I got my bachelors there last year.
Interviewer: How did you like Rutgers?
Candidate: Oh, it's a fine school. It prepared me for my graduate work.

Interviewer: Yes, I see here you went to Columbia University. That
while you were working for Jordan & Company. Did yo
to school in the evenings?

Candidate: Yes, I went in the evenings.

Was this interview laissez faire, structured, or strategic? The first question
tells you that the interviewer did not prepare for this interview. When you launch
into your interview with a question that you already know the answer to because
it is clearly stated on the résumé, you say to the candidate, "I'm not prepared."

The second question is an open question. Can you identify a strategic purpose for that question? Perhaps the interviewer simply wanted to get the candidate talking. That is a legitimate purpose and could lead you to believe this
might either be a structural or strategic interview.

After the candidate opened up a little in her response to the second question, the interviewer not only asked a question he already knew the answer
to, but he also answered the question for the candidate.

This interview appears to be laissez faire because it has no purpose,
no direction, and seems informal. It is clearly not structured—where's the
structure? Nor is it strategic—where's the strategy?

I've seen many interviews conducted in this manner. When managers get
no interview training, they depend on the résumé to guide them through the
interview. If this interview continues in this fashion, the manager will learn
next to nothing about the candidate.

Let's revisit the above interview as a strategic interview:

Interviewer: I see you went to Rutgers, so did I. Tell me what you enjoyed
about that school. (This is an open question that shares a bit
of information about the interviewer. It has a clear purpose:
to develop rapport with the candidate and to get the candidate
talking.)

Candidate: I enjoyed the freedom to study with top-of-the-line
professors. I also enjoyed the opportunity to intern one
summer for Jordan & Company.

Interviewer: When you say you enjoyed the freedom to study, what do you
mean? (Open question digs deeper into what the candidate
enjoyed.)

Candidate: I mean I liked not having too much structure. Many of my
classes were open seminars. That enabled me to pursue areas
of study I enjoyed, and that led me to my graduate work in
international business.

Interviewer: So you prefer to work in an environment without too much
structure? (This paraphrase is designed to clarify the kind of
work environment the candidate enjoys)

ndate: I like direction, but I also like to contribute and be part of the team.

This interview was focused on the candidate. The interviewer heard what the candidate said and responded to her, but the interviewer kept control of the interview. The candidate wanted to share her experiences in graduate school, but the interviewer was interested in the candidate's work history. The interviewer did not read off the résumé. Even in this short interview, we can predict this interviewer's strategy: to find out what kind of work environment this candidate prefers. If the company has a tightly supervised work team, this candidate might not be a good fit.

This example illustrates how carefully the interviewer must listen to the candidate's responses. Interviewing, therefore, is an advanced form of communication and listening.

HOW TO COMMUNICATE AS AN INTERVIEWER

Because we must exercise skillful communication to interview effectively, let's examine what communication is and how good listening affects the interview process.

In my book *Managing Sticky Situations at Work: Communication Secrets for Success in the Workplace*, I defined communication as *behavior that transmits meaning from one person to another.*[4]

Interviewers must address two important pieces of this definition, namely behavior and meaning. *Behavior* indicates what you see a person say or do that communicates something to you. Sometimes, however, that information may prove false. For example, if a person crosses her arms, you might think the person is cold, but in reality she is offended by something you said. This is where feedback comes into play. You must check out what you see and hear to determine if the *meaning* transmitted is accurate.

In a strategic interview, you cannot check out *everything* you see and hear. You must pick and chose what to address and what to ignore—remember the detective looking for clues. He cannot pour all his resources into every clue.

One major problem with the way all of us communicate is that we do not pay attention to what is going on around us. We are bombarded with so many stimuli that we ignore the most important things we see and hear. Those important pieces of the communication get overrun by the mundane and irrelevant. An attentive strategic interviewer understands this problem and sets her antenna on high alert for those important targets competencies. Let's look at an example.

Interviewer Jane is looking for a candidate who is a team player and who can produce results in a highly active environment.

Candidate Mark is talking about the work he did for a design company.

"I was responsible for picking the fabrics and for finding the be
dor that would satisfy customers. Whenever we had new custor
I went to see them and discussed their needs. Because I love art
color, I enjoyed the opportunity to explore options with the customers

"How did you come up with the appropriate vendor?" Jane asks

"We have a list of vendors that we use. After I visit with the client, I go
back to my office and select the vendors."

"And you do this alone?"

"It was a small company, just me and the owner. For the most part I
worked on my own with little interference, and I liked that."

"What did you like about working independently?"

Mark smiles. "I have worked for big operations where people barely
know who you are. In my current job we work closely when needed
and separate when needed. If, for example, I am working on a big
project, and Sandi comes in with a question, I only have to motion to
her for her to realize this isn't a good time to interrupt me. Later, we'd
confer in her office."

Jane asked questions related to what the candidate told her but did so in pur-
suit of her target: the ability to produce in a team environment. She could have
looked at other issues, such as leadership, conflict management, or customer
relations, but instead she focused on her target. *Strategic communication
means not just listening for meaning but listening for just the right meaning.*

As you examine behavior and meaning in communication, you must look at
the kinds of behavior that communicate messages.

THE POWER OF NONVERBAL BEHAVIOR IN COMMUNICATION

According to landmark research done by Albert Mehrabian at UCLA in the
1960s,[5] communication comprises three distinct parts: visual, vocal, and verbal. Mehrabian and his colleagues studied thousands of people over a number
of years to uncover these three distinct parts of communication. We must note
here that Mehrabian did not include one additional part of communication in
his research: touch. Touch is an important component of communication in an
interview. What is the first thing you do when you meet someone for the first
time? You shake hands, right? The handshake is full of nonverbal communication: is the handshake strong, weak, sweaty? As a strategic interviewer, you
want to capture that information as well as the visual, vocal, and verbal data.

When Mehrabian examined visual, vocal, and verbal communication, he
found that visual communication gave the message more power than did
vocal communication, and vocal gave the message more power than did
verbal. He discovered that we transmit meaning via each of these three portals
at differing levels of intensity. In other words, if you tell me, for example,

glad to meet you," but your eyes wander as if searching for some-
I don't believe you are glad to meet me.

n we talk about visual communication, we mean *all the* messages you
rough the eyes: gestures, facial expressions, eye contact, and personal
earance. Mehrabian found that 55 percent of communication came
ough visual messages. Since Mehrabian's research there have been inter-
sting studies that take his results a step further. The BBC Science and Nature
project, for instance, conducted a widespread study to identify fake smiles.[6]
This study gave us more information to help us sharpen our ability to read visual communication. Take a look at the site. See how many fake smiles you
can pinpoint and what leads you to believe a smile is real or fake.

Malcolm Gladwell's book *Blink* is full of information about the power of
the visual message. His premise is that we size people up—sometimes fairly
accurately—with a blink. He cites studies by John Gottman. In these studies
Gottman claimed to predict marital success. Gladwell wrote that Gottman
looked for indirect traces of emotion, for example, "that flit across one person's face; the hint of stress picked up by the sweat glands of the palm; a sud-
den surge of heart rate."[7] Gottman examined these unconscious physical
phenomena to help people determine their compatibility. He was looking
for visual messages to measure the predictability of whether a marriage
would succeed or fail, and he did so with amazing accuracy.

By *vocal communication* Mehrabian meant all the sounds we make that are
not actual words (including silence): *um*'s, sighs, laughs, chuckles, grunts,
groans. Vocal communication also includes articulation, modulation, and pac-
ing. Mehrabian found that 38 percent of communication came through the ears.
In Chapter 2 we will examine how to conduct effective interviews by telephone. Vocal communication plays a significant role when you cannot grasp
the visual message. Awareness of your vocal messages and the vocal messages
others transmit to you will help you uncover the "hidden" messages inherent in
all communication, that is, what people are not saying. *The essence of the strategic interview is to uncover those hidden messages and pursue them doggedly.*

By *verbal communication* Mehrabian meant the actual words or the content
of the message, for instance, the grammar and the word choice. Mehrabian
found that only 7 percent of communication came through the content. Even
though Mehrabian showed us that a small percentage of the power of communication comes through the words, strategic interviewers must stay aware of
the words in order to stay tuned to their key targets.

Confident communicators hear the words, and they heed the nonverbal cues.
From those cues they discover the feelings behind the words. You must become
a confident communicator to determine what lies beneath the surface. If you
interview on the surface level, you are not conducting a strategic interview.
*The only way to get under the message—to uncover the truth—is to explore what
the candidate is not saying with her words but is saying with her actions.*

Ninety-three percent of the power of the message comes through nor communication (the combination of the visual and vocal).

How does an interviewer explore nonverbal meaning? When the candid crosses his arms during the interview, do you stop and ask, "Why did you cr your arms?" When a candidate's eyes shift to the clock, do you ask, "What mac you look at the clock just now?" You cannot directly ask about a nonverbal behavior. All of us respond nonverbally on a subconscious level. That means we do not wish for these messages to come into our consciousness. Strategic interviewers must see these nonverbal cues and then address the feelings behind the action.

Let's examine an example and see how a strategic interviewer might uncover what's behind the nonverbal cues. You are recruiting a candidate for human resources manager in a large company.

> Mr. Jones, dressed in a navy suit with a colorful tie, with gray hair and carrying a briefcase, walks into your office for an interview. The man shakes your hand firmly and greets you with a smile but no eye contact. His eyes take in the surroundings in one quick movement. He sits across from you, crosses one leg over the other and glances out the window behind your desk. He straightens the crease in his pants as you begin the interview. His fingers thump the top of his briefcase while you talk.

List everything you take in about this man before he says one word.

- Dresses carefully (this interview is important to him)
- Firm handshake (confidence)
- No eye contact at handshake (nervous or closed personality or impatient)
- Glances out the window before talking, not looking at you (nervous, gathering himself). If you hear a vocal cue such as a sigh, you can confirm he is anxious to get this interview over. Perhaps he knows you are the first step in a series of interviews.
- Straightens the crease in his pants (not looking at you, more concerned about the impression he's making, attention to detail)
- Fingers thump the top of his briefcase while you talk (anxious, in a hurry, impatient)

How the Interviewer Might Interview Mr. Jones

If you find yourself face to face with Mr. Jones, here are some tips to enable you to gain control of the interview:

- Begin the interview as an orientation. Let the candidate know what he'll be going through and with whom he will meet. Spend the first few minutes before you begin asking questions. Do not get defensive. Do list credentials or compete for the man's respect. You know from non-al behaviors that he's confident, nervous, and perhaps in a h. You so know he's impatient. He wants to get on with the process a perhaps interview with the big wigs.

The man seems tense; you should relax. Ask questions that get candidate talking. Listen intently to what he says and respond without h probing.

- If he's still showing signs of impatience or nervousness aft you've begun talking, address those signs gently: "I've noticed you se a bit restless. Could I get you a cup of coffee or some bottled water?"
- Watch the candidate's visual cues for changes. When relaxes, ask the more probing questions.
- Don't let the candidate's tension rub off on you. Your goal is to create a safe environment in which your relaxed demeanor will rub off on him, not the reverse.

As this example illustrates, we can learn a lot from just a few nonverbal messages. How you respond to those messages will determine the success of the interview. If, for example, you responded defensively to Mr. Jones—his nonverbal cues suggested he didn't want to be talking with you—you would lose out.

THE POWER OF PERCEPTION IN THE INTERVIEW

Perception plays an important and often obscure role in the interview. Strategic interviewers can do all the right things and still get sidetracked by perception. What is perception, and how does it affect the interview?

I defined perception in my first book on strategic interviewing as *an unidentified feeling that is not based on fact.*[8]

Imagine this familiar scenario: A candidate walks into your office for an interview. You've reviewed the résumé and carefully isolated the strategic issues you want to address. You've also studied the job and know what is needed. Indeed, you've done all your homework. As soon as the candidate walks in, you get a bad vibe. You shake the candidate's hand, and you still feel uncomfortable. As you go through the interview, a voice in the back of your head screams, "No!" You try to listen to the candidate, but in the end, you know you cannot hire this person. The vibes are too strong. When the candidate leaves, you realize you didn't hear most of what he said, and you have no idea why you don't like him, but you don't.

In this case you made the right decision not to hire. Strategic interviewers do all they can to counteract the power of perception, but *if the perception persists, the best course of action is to go with your gut.* What have you lost if you do so? You may have let a very good candidate slip by. But you do know that. What you do know is if you take a risk and hire, you may make a costly hiring mistake. It is less costly to reject this candidate and go on to the next one than to hire. Perception in this case has won.

Let's look at another scenario. This time the candidate walks in, and from the moment she enters the room, there's instant rapport. Again, you've done your homework, studied the résumé, isolated the key target areas, and planned your interview. But this time, the little voice in the back of your head is saying, "Yes!" In whatever way the candidate responds, your mind says, "great answer." Once again you try and go through your planned strategic interview, probing for key points, but you find yourself skipping parts because you know you're going to offer this person the job. After all, she is perfect. Right?

Wrong! In this case you made the wrong decision. When you have a positive perception about someone, you are in dangerous territory. Your listening ability diminishes. Whatever the candidate says, even if she says something outrageous, you give her the benefit of the doubt. The candidate wins you over with her ability to "snow" you. There are many candidates out there who are extremely skilled at interviewing. Even seasoned interviewers fall prey to these perception traps. In this case, you've failed to answer the ultimate question: can this candidate do the job? The positive perception clouded your judgment. But, you say, wasn't your judgment clouded by the negative perception as well? Of course it was. The bottom line lies in the cost in making an incorrect decision. *When the perception is negative and you decide not to hire, the cost is negligible, but when the perception is positive and you decide to hire, the cost is enormous.*

How can a strategic interviewer manage perception? Awareness is half the battle. You must recognize when you've been zapped by a perception, either positive or negative. Now that you understand that the most dangerous perceptions are positive, you can be on high alert when you've been zapped by positive perceptions. In other words you cannot accept your own judgment when your perceptions are too strong. You must call for reinforcements. Ask a colleague to join the interview, and conduct it as a team. We will discuss team interviews in Chapter 4. Be careful, however. Perceptions are contagious. If you tell your colleague, "I really like this person, and it's clouding my judgment," you have immediately shared the perception virus. Instead, simply say to your colleague you need another opinion. You need not explain further.

In this chapter we've defined strategic interviews by looking at the history of interviewing and contrasting a strategic focus with laissez-faire and structured interviewing. We've also taken a long look at communication and the impact of nonverbal cues on the interview decision. Finally we examined the power of perception in order to prepare ourselves for perception landmines.

Chapter 2 we'll look at the way strategic interviewers recruit candidates. ther words, how do you get the right people to interview in the first place? ring smart begins before the candidate actually walks through your door. It egins with the initial decision to open up the recruiting process.

PRACTICE EXERCISE

Read the following interview and identify whether the interview is strategic, structured, or laissez faire:

Interviewer: Thank you for coming in today. My name is Martha Lewis and I'm going to spend just a few minutes talking to you today before we continue with the interview process. Let's begin with getting to know one another a little. Tell me about yourself.

Candidate: I grew up here in Kalamazoo, and I love living here. Even though I went out of town to college, I'm anxious to get back here where my family lives and all.

Interviewer: I grew up here too. I left to study in California for a few years but it didn't take me long to realize I needed to get back. My gosh people out there in California are different, if you know what I mean.

Candidates: (laughs) I do know what you mean. My roommate at college was from San Francisco. I thought she was great, but I have to say, she was really different.

Interviewer: Sort of like a modern day hippie?

Candidate: Yeah. She wore the strangest clothes and practiced yoga in the room every day. I did start drinking herbal tea, but that's about as far as I got.

Interviewer: What kind of herbal tea?

Was this interview strategic, structured, or laissez faire? (See Appendix A for answers.)

TWO

Recruiting: Finding the Right People to Apply

In Chapter 1 we defined interviewing. Specifically we contrasted laissez-faire interviewing with structured interviewing with strategic interviewing. We also learned the importance of communication, listening, and perceptions on the interview process. These factors set the foundation for interviewing smart. But before you ask that first question, there are steps you need to take to accomplish your goal to hire smart and keep 'em.

The first part of the POINT process is P for planning. What do you plan, and how do you get the right people to come through the door to interview? The answers to these questions fall under the umbrella of recruiting.

Most interviewing processes include a recruiting plan. This plan encompasses the following:

- Writing quality job descriptions that describe the job
- Culling out the target competencies—soft skills for doing the job
- Identifying where to locate your best candidates, including online sites
- Screening résumés with a strategic purpose
- Identifying the best medium for screening candidates, including virtual modes.

HOW TO WRITE A QUALITY JOB DESCRIPTION

The simplest way to examine how to write a job description is to ask yourself one basic question: does the description you wrote describe the job? *Most job descriptions do not describe the job.* To illustrate this point, here's an example of a job description for a business manager.

This job requires special people with unique qualities to drive our innovation and business development activities. The person will report to the Business Manager. The successful candidate should have the following orientation:

- Be passionate about driving innovation and change
- Display high energy and be fully committed to the role, its opportunities and challenges
- Show tenacity and durability to break down the barriers of change
- Be creative in collecting insights and converting them into novel solutions, while quickly closing non-value-added challenges
- Have the ability to collaborate both internally and externally to shape ideas and concepts and to communicate them successfully in order to build a robust development portfolio.

Tell me what the person in the above job description does. What are her duties? If you were applying for this job, would you have a clear picture of what the job entails and whether or not you might be able to do it? The answer to these questions is a resounding *No!* The above job description does not describe the job; instead it describes the kind of person the company is looking for to do the job. *Describing the job and describing the person are two very different components.* To develop a smart recruiting plan, you need both. First, you need to know what duties are required to do the job. Second, you need to know what skills are necessary to be successful in the job. The first part—the duties required—comprise the job description. The second part—the skills necessary to do the job—comprise the target competencies. Dan Erling in *Match* divided these two phases of the recruiting plan as follows: Phase one includes "Compiling the Job Overview," that is, the job description and the skills required. Phase two includes "Creating the Competency Profile, i.e., the skills the hiring team uses to evaluate soft skills."[1] I might note here that Erling was the only source I could find that made this nice distinction. Most books lumped these two pieces together, and hence we have a lot of confusion about job descriptions.

Taking our cue from Erling, we'll look first at how to write a job description, namely what the components are and what it takes to make a job description effective, and next we'll look at soft-skill competencies needed for doing the job.

One reason today's recruiting plan must have well-written job descriptions is that recruiting in our world has gone through radical changes in the past decade. Let's examine those changes before we get into the basics of writing job descriptions.

HISTORY OF JOB DESCRIPTIONS IN TODAY'S RECRUITING ENVIRONMENT

If you happen to be a manager who has been around for more than a decade, you know that job descriptions have become a thing of the past. Believe it or not, most companies do not write job descriptions for their jobs.

In the past companies created job descriptions for two reasons: (1) auditing purposes and (2) internal organization. Over time two events happened, the first being that employees with job descriptions narrowed their view of their work responsibilities only to those listed in the job description. How many of us have heard people say, "It's not in my job description," meaning, of course, employees did not feel compelled to perform tasks outside of their job descriptions? This puts a great restraint on growth, development, and flexibility in jobs. The second event that happened to cause companies to turn away from job descriptions was that some employees or employee unions used job descriptions as the foundation for lawsuits. The natural response to both these events was to quit writing job descriptions. If a job description were written, the human resource manager often put the document away in a drawer and never referred to it again. The amount of work to create job descriptions did not justify their existence.

Today's recruiting landscape is very different than it was even five years ago. In the past, when a job opened up, managers placed a brief notice in the newspaper. They also scoured the professional journals and associations to identify appropriate spots for placing notices. The notice was a brief description of the job, often one or two sentences, with clear requirements before applying. Applications and résumés came from the small sample of people who read the advertisement.

The Information Age changed that landscape. Candidates began hunting for jobs online. They looked at such sites as monster.com, career.com, and theladder .com. They mined those sites to locate positions suitable to their talent, using keyword searches. Virtual recruiting emerged with three significant changes:

- Candidates find you (often using keyword searches to uncover possible jobs that may not even be open yet).
- The number of candidates who apply has grown in significant numbers to make recruiting a time-consuming burden to most managers.
- Job descriptions have assumed a prominent role in screening.

In the old days you recruited candidates. You placed ads in order to search for qualified people to fill your jobs. Today's candidates find you. They search the web until they locate companies they want to work for. They search recruiting sites for the kinds of jobs they want and position themselves for those jobs. This puts a lot of responsibility for recruiting in the hands of the candidates.

Furthermore, in the past you had a lot of résumés when you received hundreds for a single job posting. Today, most openings receive thousands of résumés. Not only has the job market tightened but also the number of people with access to information has grown exponentially over the years. This means the manager may have to sift through a mountain of résumés to find the right people to interview. Is that how you want to spend your time? *To hire smart you must find ways to use your recruiting time more efficiently.*

Finally, the job postings that characterized our listings in the old days are a thing of the past. *Today's world requires clear, professionally written job descriptions to help sort through the many candidates who have eyes on your openings.* Essentially the job description becomes your first brush at screening, and the people doing the screening are not the managers but the candidates. Your job description must tell the candidate enough to know whether this is a job he wants to do and whether he's qualified to interview for that job. Job descriptions must be clear enough for candidates to ascertain whether or not they are a fit but can't be so detailed that it restricts job performance.

COMPONENTS OF A JOB DESCRIPTION FOR THE TWENTY-FIRST CENTURY

Today's job descriptions have two major components: *description of the job* and *qualifications.*

Describing the job consists of three parts:

1. Summary Statement
2. Duties
3. Tasks

Summary Statement Defined

This statement provides a general overview of the job and how it fits within the company. It includes the basic parameters of the job, namely work location, to whom the position reports, and hours. If the job is highly professional, you need not include hours.

Example: Sales Manager Position

This position is responsible for the sales operations in the northeast assigned by the general sales manager, to whom this position reports. The work location is the regional office in Boston, Massachusetts. The workdays and hours are Monday through Friday from 8 a.m. to 5 p.m. This position requires 80 percent time on the road.

Comment

A prospective candidate reading this summary statement may opt not to apply simply due to the amount of travel. Another candidate may choose to apply because Boston is where she wants to live.

Duties Defined

Duties encompass major subdivisions of the work responsibility. Most job descriptions have three to four duties associated with them. Duties consist of the major chunks in a job, not every little thing a person does.

Example: Sales Manager
- Sales supervision: Leads a field sales team that sells marketing solutions to customers within their local market.
- Sales Management: Coordinates the prospecting, sale, service, and account assignment of clients. Leads the team within the organization to optimize use of company departments and resources to exceed sales revenues and goals.
- Account Strategy: Meets or exceeds revenue goals through a team-based, consultative approach to sales.

Comment

Prospective candidates who have had no sales experience will not fully understand these duties and will likely screen themselves out. Others, who understand sales, might screen themselves out because they might not wish to take responsibility for a sales team. Many salespeople are loners who prefer to work on their own and be accountable for their own selling.

Tasks Defined

Tasks comprise a single work operation that is an essential step to perform a duty. The job description need not list all tasks but a sufficient number to adequately describe the duties associated with that job.

Tasks define the methods, procedures, and techniques by which duties are carried out.

- What is done (action)
- How it is done (procedures, materials, tools, or equipment)
- Why it is done (purpose)

Example: Sales Manager Position
Duty: Sales Supervision

Tasks:

- Lead sales team meetings to coordinate sales efforts and simulate new sales strategies.
- Create multiproduct marketing solutions that include innovative uses of social media.
- Communicate changes in direction, products, expectations, processes, and standards both up and down the chain of command in order to prevent missteps or overlapping duties.

Duty: Sales Management

- Ensure consistent adherence to standardized sales processes to maintain the corporate brand.
- Review sales proposals in advance to ensure that clients receive the appropriate products, services and rates.

Duty: Account Strategy

- Manage account assignments and sales leads across a variety of media sales channels in order to maximize market share and revenue.
- Facilitate account-specific strategic planning to maximize market share and revenue and increase the potential of team's account lists.
- Assign accounts to appropriate sales channels with consideration to shared growth, cost of sale, and client potential across team members.
- Maintain ongoing coordination to monitor sales performance, forecasting, and account reassignment in order to lead the team to the highest standard of results.

Comment

These duties and tasks provide enough information for a prospective candidates to screen themselves out but not so much that they limit job performance. Some companies add a final duty at the end of all job descriptions: *Carry out all tasks related to this job that might increase individual and team job performance.*

Specifying the qualifications includes the knowledge, skills, and abilities the candidate must have to perform the job.

- Knowledge: The level of education, experience, and training an individual must have to be considered qualified for the position.
- Skills: Specific skills such as ability to create, manipulate, and utilize spreadsheets, word processing programs, and so on (avoid using program names unless knowledge of that specific program is essential).

- Abilities: Those physical or other abilities a person must have to do the job. These include ability to lift certain weights, ability to manipulate heavy equipment, and ability to drive large vehicles.

Comment

Managers must decide when writing the qualifications whether the qualification is required or preferred. If you do not wish to train candidates to do a certain thing—in other words, if you want the person to have the knowledge or skill ahead of time—then the qualification is *required*. If you are willing to train the candidate in a certain knowledge or skill, then that qualification is *preferred*.

Example: Sales Manager
Required
- Knowledge: Three years business-to-business field sales experience with quotas. Three years media sales or advertising industry experience. Two years sales management experience. High school diploma, GED, or equivalent work experience
- Skills: Working knowledge of Windows-based PCs, Microsoft Office

Preferred
- Knowledge: BA degree from a four-year college or university. Four years experience leading sales teams.
- Skills: Use of social media with a strong database in sites like LinkedIn or Facebook with over 1,000 connections.

Note: For professional positions, job descriptions often do not include specific abilities.

TIPS FOR WRITING CLEAR, PROFESSIONAL JOB DESCRIPTIONS

The following tips will help you create a job description that not only enable candidates to screen themselves in or out but will also help launch your company toward a professional recruiting plan.

- Be precise. Keep sentence structure as simple as possible; omit unnecessary words that do not contribute pertinent information.
- Be clear. The requirements listed on the job description must support the essential functions of the job and serve as the primary criteria for selecting or rejecting candidates. In other words, if you list requirements as "required," you cannot change your mind.
- Begin each duty or task with an *action verb* in the *present tense*—the here and now. Take a look at Appendix B for examples of action verbs. The

reason quality job descriptions use action verbs is to give them clarity. Action verbs show an action. For example instead of using a "to be" verb (*is, are, was, were*), use a verb that shows action, such as *leads, coordinates*, or *writes*. With these verbs you can see what the person does.

- Be consistent when using terms like *may* and *occasionally*. Job descriptions isolate the primary responsibilities the person does. Avoid secondary responsibilities that fall in the category of "may" or "occasionally."

- Refer to job titles rather than incumbents, for instance "Reports to Sales Manager" instead of "Reports to Mary Smith." You may think this tip obvious, but remember that job descriptions were primarily used for internal use. For that reason many refer to people versus position titles. If you think you can get away with pulling one of those descriptions out of the drawer and dusting it off, you'll have lots of dusting to do!

- Use a logical sequence in describing duties and responsibilities, and be consistent.

- Don't lock yourself into strict requirements that may prevent you from considering qualified candidates. For example, instead of saying, "required: master of science degree in industrial engineering," consider substitutions such as "master's degree or a minimum of six to eight years of relevant professional experience."

- Define uncommon abbreviations. Avoid jargon that only people in a certain field or profession understand. Even though you might argue that jargon would screen out certain candidates, it also shows a lack of professionalism.

- Avoid phrases such as *assist in, responsible for*, and *involved in* when writing duties and tasks. You can use these general terms when writing the summary statement (which, of course, is more general).

Finally, when thinking about constructing your job description, imagine an inverted pyramid. The summary statement is more general, the duties less so, and the tasks even less so. By the time candidates finish reading the full description, they have a good idea of what the job entails.

CULLING OUT THE TARGET COMPETENCIES: SOFT SKILLS FOR DOING THE JOB

Now that you have a clear job description in hand, you can move on to the second part of a smart recruiting plan: identifying the soft skills for doing the job. Note the job description contains no soft skills because soft skills are vague and job descriptions are precise. So, what is a soft skill?

Soft skills are the communication, listening, managerial, and leadership skills needed for achieving success on the job. They are the fuzzy things people

EXAMPLE OF A COMPLETE JOB DESCRIPTION:
COMPUTER TRAINING ASSOCIATE

Responsible for delivering seminars in locations assigned by the general training manager, to whom this position reports. The training targets 40 divisions of the company and 400 specific administrative employees. Duties include the design and delivery of computer workshops and one-on-one instruction of new software packages. The work location is in the regional office in Tampa, Florida, Monday through Friday from 8 a.m. to 5 p.m. This position requires 80 percent time on the road.

Provides direct computer training workshops to internal teams:

- Interacts with internal teams to create computer training programs to meet their particular needs.
- Delivers seminars of one- to two-day duration related to all areas of computing services, and particularly related to data entry, word processing, technical writing, and quality assurance.
- Provides one-on-one instruction to acquaint administrative staff with new software packages.
- Follows up with internal clients to identify additional computing training needs both one-on-one and in groups.

Creates new programs:

- Researches the methods for program delivery best suited to the topic being taught.
- Tests new activities for delivery in the classroom to maximize learning.
- Designs the agenda, handout materials, and PowerPoint programs inherent with each seminar.
- Creates training manuals for self-instruction.

Leads team training:

- Represents the computing area throughout the company.
- Designs and implements innovative software into the team training experience to vary the learning experience.
- Supervises the delivery of the aspects of training related to computing when working with others in the company.

QUALIFICATIONS

Required:

- High school diploma
- Four-year degree in an area related to computer science or computing or five years experience with hands-on computer technology
- Two years experience as a managing supervisor of three to five employees

Preferred:

- College degree in computer science
- Two years experience in delivering computer training
- Skill with major spreadsheet software and word processing software
- Skill in software and hardware systems that use DOS
- Ability to write manuals

do in their interactions with one another, hence the term "soft." As an interviewer you must probe to determine if the person has the proven ability to accomplish certain soft skills. Determining whether someone has the "hard" skills to do a job is easy. In other words, if a person graduated with honors with a chemistry degree from a reputable university, you need not probe whether she knows how to run tests in a laboratory. If a person finished a two-year community college program on the uses of computer software, you need not probe her ability to use Microsoft Office. If you have concerns about these kinds of skills, you can easily make a determination through written testing without interviewing. *We employ the skills of strategic interviewing to uncover the soft skills.* For example, you must determine if a person who may have solid technical skills (hard skills) can communicate how to use the software to nonusers (soft skills). Erling says, "the hard skills can be taught, but soft skills touch on a basic approach to work. You can't teach these kinds of skills."[2] I disagree with Erling on one count. We can teach the soft skills, but we do not. Why? For the same reasons we ignore teaching interviewing skills in our business schools. We assume they are intuitive, or we write them off as too difficult to teach. One thing we do know: soft skills are harder to isolate and quantify than hard skills and therefore harder to ascertain in an interview.

Table 2.1 shows a way to define soft skills.

Table 2.1 An Example of How to Quantify Soft Skills

Competency	Description	Key Behaviors	Probes
• Communication	• Expresses ideas clearly in individual and group situations with all levels of people	• Expresses thoughts and ideas • Uses nonverbal cues to punctuate messages • Gives more than yes/no answers • Asks questions • Uses listening skills to demonstrate comprehension • Has good eye contact	• How do you express your ideas to others as (a particular role)? • Give me an example of how you know when someone is listening to you. • Before you made your last presentation, what steps did you take?
• Leadership Skills (People)	• Directs and models company values to achieve results	• Directs others to achieve goals • Actively involves in leadership roles; holds leadership positions • Easily deals with conflict • Works side-by-side with others to achieve team goals	• When you were (a particular leadership role), how did you get results? • Describe how you dealt with conflict when you were (a particular leadership role). • Give an example of how you have achieved results through teamwork.
• Problem Solving	• Creates innovative solutions with analytical methods using multiple resources	• Analyzes facts to reach innovative solutions • Sees opportunities in new ideas • Uses multiple resources, old and new, to reach innovative solutions	• How did you go about selecting (your school, your major, your career)? • When existing systems did not work for you (in a particular situation), what did you do? • Tell me how you went about solving (a particular problem).

(continued)

Table 2.1 (continued)

Competency	Description	Key Behaviors	Probes
• Professionalism	• Conducts business in a manner consistent with the company goals and values	• Dresses consistently with a job interview situation • Seeks opportunities for self-improvement • Speaks with strong voice and steady eye contact • Sets and achieves high goals • Is prepared for the interview with résumé in hand	• Give me an example of what you do when things at work don't go your way. • When you worked for (a particular job or leadership role at school), how did you present your points in order to get the results you wanted? • Share an example of how you set and achieved a particular goal.

The following is an example of how to make the soft skill "ability to lead" less soft:

Interviewer: When you worked for Smith's Company, how did you get your team to accomplish its goals?

Candidate: I saw my job as a motivator. I didn't force the team to do anything. Instead I encouraged through example.

Interviewer: How do you encourage people through example?

Candidate: Once when we were struggling to make our target, I joined the team for a weekend long marathon of work. We all pitched in, and after that weekend, we exceeded our target.

Interviewer: So you're saying you're willing to join in and work with the team when necessary?

Leadership defined by this candidate means motivating others to do the job. The interviewer went further to uncover how the candidate defined motivation. In so doing, the soft skill "leadership" became clearer.

WHERE TO FIND THE BEST CANDIDATES

Like everything else we do in a strategic interview, identifying where to find our best candidates cannot be structured. Companies must address each job differently. Most companies, however, recruit for similar jobs. For example, if your company is an accounting company, you tend to hire accountants and bookkeepers. If your company is a manufacturing company, you tend to hire engineers and business executives. Let's look at some of the typical places where you can target your recruiting efforts:

- Colleges and universities. Target those institutions where you've had the greatest success with employees. If your best hires have come out of local technical schools, focus your recruiting there. If your best hires have come from particular four-year institutions, focus there. The question is not where you think the "smartest" people are. *The question is which college or university or other institution produces the best fit for your jobs.*

- Online sites. Just like with colleges and universities, you want to target those online job sites where you've found the best people. If you have never used online sites to generate interest in your jobs, I suggest you start with some of the largest: monster.com or careerbuilder.com. Make sure you post good, solid job descriptions. If you want to narrow your search, you can post jobs on sites related to particular fields, for example, engineerjobs.com or accounting.com. Monster.com also allows you to narrow your search by posting by career. You can also post jobs on the online boards of many professional associations.

- LinkedIn.com. LinkedIn holds the title as the largest professional social networking site with over 100 million users. Surveys show that nearly 60 percent of those users have high personal incomes and hold positions of executive level or higher.[3] LinkedIn began as a job search resource and an important recruiting tool. Headhunters as well as human resource professionals use LinkedIn to identify potential candidates. Through a strong LinkedIn group of connections, 500 connections or more, you can position yourself to network with people in a similar field. This network provides a wealth of opportunity for recruiting worldwide. LinkedIn groups also provide a resource for job posting. Each specialized group has a place for people to either post jobs or to post their interest in being recruited. If, for example, you are a member of the sales and marketing group on LinkedIn and your company is searching for sales associates, posting on this site provides a good way to unearth high-quality candidates.

- Headhunters. Headhunters help companies hire people. Their goal is to help you fill your jobs with the best people. They often know of people who are looking for a career move but who do not wish to browse the web or to actively engage in a search.

These options suggest ways to bring people to you. Remember, however, that in today's market candidates find you either through LinkedIn, your own website, or active blogging.

Your next step is to screen candidates to determine whom you wish to interview. Headhunters help with the screening process, but even they do not make the final choice. *One of the biggest problems in many companies is relying too heavily on headhunters or internal human resource managers to make the choice.* Indeed, when a human resource manager or a headhunter brings you a candidate, she must not share her bias. No matter how much credence you give her judgment, you must not allow anyone to color the process, either pro or con, particularly in the screening stage. Beware the dangers of perceptions. You must guard against being swayed by either your perceptions or those of others.

THE SCREENING PROCESS

When looking at your strategic recruiting plan, you must distinguish between the interview process and the screening process. *The recruiting plan encompasses everything you need to do to get the best candidates through the door for an interview.* Hence recruitment includes everything that leads up to the interview. Screening is the final step in the recruiting plan after developing the job description, culling out the competencies, and posting your job.

At this stage you've written a quality job description, which you have posted in strategic locations in both the real and virtual worlds. Now you must narrow the field and reduce the number of people who actually enter the interview process.

Step 1

Go through the résumés. Begin with what you required in the job description and make two piles: those people who meet the requirements and those people who do not. Once that is completed, examine what you listed for preferred skills. Again, make two piles: those who have your preferred qualifications and those who do not.

Step 2

Study the résumés you have left, and rule out any who do not fit your needs. The following examples illustrate things you could rule out:

- People who have had short-term lengths of service, if loyalty and longevity are things your company values.
- Size of companies the person worked for that are not congruent with your company.
- People who attended colleges or universities that do not have strong curricula in a field you need.
- People who have made blatant errors on their résumés.

Step 3

Go to your list of competencies. If one of your competencies is teamwork, but you note on the résumé that the person worked independently and never played any team sports, you might rule out that candidate. If leadership is a competency you're looking for, but you note the person never served in a leadership capacity either in his job or in his professional organizations, you might rule out that person.

Once you've accomplished these three steps, you have culled the résumés down to a group of people who appear to fit your position as closely as you can ascertain from the résumé alone. The next step is to conduct a screening interview.

HOW TO CONDUCT A SCREENING INTERVIEW

The following two questions will help you prepare for the screening interview:

1. What knowledge and skills match those you're looking for?
2. What gaps or red flags do you see on the résumé?

Remember the point of the screening interview is not to determine if the person is perfect for the job. Instead, you want to determine if the person qualifies for a strategic interview. If you represent a small business and you're the only person interviewing, you may want to combine the screening and the strategic interview into one step. Otherwise, you must recognize the limitations of the screening interview versus a true strategic interview.

What are the differences between a screening interview and a final strategic interview?

- The screening interview focuses broadly on a many competencies. The final interview focuses narrowly on one or two major competencies.
- The screening interview is usually shorter—15 to 20 minutes—while a final interview lasts from 30 to 45 minutes.
- The screening interview screens. It does not decide to hire or not.
- The screening interview may be conducted by telephone or virtually either on Skype or other webcam-based video technology.[4]

Note you must conduct final strategic interviews face-to-face. You lose too much communication when you interview by telephone or virtually. Although webcam-based communication provides visual information, the slight delay in the communication distorts the message. Remembering the importance of nonverbal cues, you must acknowledge the limitations of these methods and use them only for screening purposes. Choosing the correct medium for interviewing is part of the recruiting plan.

Tips for Telephone Screening

- Pay unusually close attention to the verbal and vocal cues because telephone screening eliminates the visual cues,
- Do not script your call. Just like with all strategic interviewing, you want a candidate-focused call. Once you examine the résumé and isolate what target competencies you wish to probe, focus on those points. These will vary from candidate to candidate. For example, you may have a candidate who has been active in a number of professional organizations, serving as president in everything he belonged to. You need not screen this candidate on leadership, but you would do so with others who do not have such strong leadership indicators on their résumés.
- Clarify all deal-breakers (those items that would mean a definite not hire). If the candidate left off important information on the résumé, get that

information first. For example, if being able to handle large-scale machinery is not noted on the résumé but is required in the job, ask that question early in the screening interview.

- Make sure you use the communication skills of a strategic interview even though you are performing a screening interview—that is, use the intentional listening skills: probe, paraphrase, summarize, flipside, reality-test, and reflect (see Chapters 7 through 9) and quality behavior-based questions (see Chapter 3).
- Listen for silences. Note fillers, *um*'s, and *ah*'s.
- Note qualifiers in communication such as, "I think" or "I believe." These suggest a lack of confidence.
- Note if the person talks too much or not enough.
- How much energy do you hear in the person's voice? When you ask about certain things, does the voice drop or rise with enthusiasm? A drop in voice suggests a lack of interest and hints at what a person enjoys doing versus what she prefers delegating.
- Do not use your cell phone. There's a delay in communication on a cell phone that distorts sensitive vocal communication. When possible, use your landline.
- Do not use a speaker phone where vocal messages are also distorted. People sound as if they are talking in a tunnel. Furthermore, the candidate has no idea how many people might be listening to the response. This unknown can bias the conversation. If you wish to conduct a team interview by phone, use a dedicated bridge line where all the callers are identified.

Drawbacks for Screening Using Skype or Google Talk

- The visual picture on Skype is distorted. You cannot see the small nuances that provide important visual information, namely, a shoulder shrug, a blink of an eye, or how the person is dressed.
- Because communication by Skype is delayed, the visual and vocal responses are delayed. For example, if you say something funny, the person does not laugh until a few seconds later. This delay makes it hard to determine if the visual messages are aligned with the verbal messages.
- Skype's visual is often blurry or snowy at best. You can get a general picture of the person, but if you had to determine specifics, such as maintaining eye contact, it might be harder. Facial details are difficult to see.

Tips for Using Skype or Google Talk

Use any of the webcam-based visual communication channels for candidate screening, not for the final interview process. These tools are excellent resources for you to "see" a candidate, personalize the interview, and determine if the candidate is a fit for further interviewing. As noted, both Skype and Google Talk offer very similar services, and I discuss them here interchangeably. Choose the service that best suits your needs.

- Get comfortable with the technology. Practice before you make that first interview call. Look at yourself on the webcam. Get a colleague to Skype you and give you feedback about sound.
- Use the best equipment, including a professional microphone and broadband Ethernet connections. Do not use Wi-Fi unless there is no other choice. Test the speed beforehand. You can do that at www.speedtest.net.
- Dress professionally from head to toe. So why dress from head to toe when the candidate will only see you from the chest up? If you have to stand during the interview, you want the candidate to see you in appropriate dress (not your pajamas or shorts).
- If you work in a cubicle or at home, go to a place that is quiet. For cubicle workers, go to a conference room. If you work at home, find a quiet spot where others won't interrupt the call. Don't try to interview someone on a laptop or iPad in a busy place, such as an airport.
- Be sure the visual background is appropriate. It's best to have little or no background. You may distort the visual message when there are distractions such as strange photos or unusual plants in the background.
- If you use headsets, test them beforehand. Again, try to anticipate malfunctions in technology.
- Place your camera in a spot where you can look directly at the screen and *it appears as if you're looking in the eye of the camera*. If you look at the camera and not the screen, you'll miss important visual cues. But you do not want your eyes moving around or not looking at the candidate.
- Finally, check out the tips for interviewing on Skype at www.skype.com. You'll learn what Skype advises job-seeking candidates to do. Those who do their homework will have studied that site.

Tips for What to Watch For on a Webcam Interview

- Watch the way the person listens to your questions. Because of the delay in the verbal and visual signals, you have an excellent opportunity to watch how a person listens.
- Pay attention to how the person responds to your questions. Use all the tips for telephone interviews, but include visual cues as well.
- Note if the person has visual habits that distract from the communication, namely, excessive touching of their face or hair, wiggling around in the seat,

or nibbling on fingernails. Some visual issues may be the result of the technology. For example, most people lean in to hear the speaker. Even if they use earphones, they often lean in toward the screen.

- Listen for nervous laughter, laughter that seems inappropriate given the situation.

- Note how the person articulates. Does he swallow words, making it hard for you to understand his responses?

Finally, when screening by telephone or with web-based technology, your job is to gather enough information to determine the next steps. Be sure to give the candidate information about how to follow up. Be specific and clear and then follow up as promised.

In this chapter we explored how get the right people through the door to interview by creating a strong recruiting plan. That plan includes well-written job descriptions, clear identification of the target competencies (soft skills), posting the job descriptions in strategic locations, and screening candidates both by résumé and later in a screening interview, either face-to-face, by telephone, or via web-based technology. We differentiated between the screening interview and the final strategic interview.

In Chapter 3 we will begin to lay the foundation for conducting strategic interviews starting with behavior-based interviewing.

PRACTICE EXERCISE: HOW TO WRITE A STRATEGIC RECRUITING PLAN

Answer *True* or *False* to the following questions.

1. Job descriptions need not be precise, but a general description of what you're looking for.

2. There are two major components of a job description: The description of the job and qualifications.

3. The job description includes all competencies—hard and soft skills.

4. The ability to work with people should be included in the job description in jobs that deal with the public.

5. It's a good idea to post your job everywhere you can.

6. Abilities and knowledge are the same kinds of qualifications.

7. A screening interview can be conducted on web-based visual channels such as Skype.

8. Final interviews may be conducted by telephone.

See Appendix A for answers.

THREE

Using Behavior-Based Interviewing

In Chapter 2 we looked at everything you need to do to prepare for a strategic interview. The P in the POINT process stands for *plan*. We began with the job description and the components of a job description, including a clear summary statement, precise duties and tasks, as well as both required and preferred qualifications. We also isolated the soft skills necessary to succeed on the job. Finally we looked at where to post the job and how to screen résumés and candidates. Presumably you are ready to launch your strategic interview. Wait! Not so quick. We have a few more items to clarify before that interview begins.

One of the most important aspects of hiring smart is to ask questions that reveal whether or not the person can do the job. Unfortunately, many managers do not do that. Instead they ask irrelevant questions or questions that tell them nothing about performance.

Behavior-based questioning brings you closer to revealing whether a person can do a job than any other form of questioning. Remember that the best way to tell whether or not a person can do the job is for him or her to actually do it. That's the foolproof method for ascertaining performance. In reality, you often do not (and sometimes never) have that option. Unless your company has a strong co-op program or intern program, you cannot watch a potential candidate do the job. And even in those cases, many companies wish to bring on qualified co-ops. In other words, even with co-ops, you want to hire smart. So how does behavior-based interviewing help you learn if the person can perform?

Behavior-based interviewing focuses on a person's *past* behavior. The theory behind this kind of interviewing is that *the best predictor of a person's behavior is what they've done in the past*. Dr. Pierre Mornell called this his maxim, but I believe it has been around for many years, and some may consider it common sense. Much of management and leadership comes from commonsense ideas. Sometimes, however, as managers we do not apply our commonsense knowledge when dealing with people. Mornell did so, and confirmed this maxim many times over during 40 years of psychiatric experience. He said, "If a man was great with people but lousy with details in his last three jobs, you predict his future behavior accordingly."[1] How many of you, however, believe that given the right conditions or the right resources, he will change?

Mornell went on to caution us, "Everyone makes mistakes in their career, and sometimes bad things (or bad bosses) happen to good people. It's important to recognize these human realities and to discuss them as part of the hiring process."[2] But how do you uncover the things people do not want to tell you? Few candidates willingly tell interviewers the bad things they have done in previous jobs. And not many want to bad-mouth their previous bosses (if they did, you'd probably not hire them, right?). These are the issues you strive to uncover in the strategic interview. Candidates prefer to tell you all the good stuff they've done, and they work very hard at not telling you the bad stuff. Behavior-based interviewing helps to uncover those less than stellar incidents candidates wish to keep covered up, and it does so in a nonthreatening manner.

Let's explore the difficulties of behavior-based interviewing. Most of us wish to believe that people will change. We harbor that nagging hope that given the right situation, people will perform differently (and, indeed, sometimes they do). For example, an employee who is habitually late for work may tell you that she doesn't have adequate transportation. You help her find public transportation she can use each morning to arrive on time. Nonetheless, she still arrives late. You purchase an alarm clock for her. She still arrives late. This employee may at some point change this behavior, but the likelihood is slim and the cost of waiting expensive. For all you know she's arrived late for everything she's ever done in her life.

As Mornell told us, using past behavior provides a good predictor for future behavior, but it is not the only predictor. Those occasional exceptions to the rule are what confuse us. Some of you are thinking about that one employee you took a risk on, the one everyone counseled you not to hire because of past behavior. That employee turned out to be your best hiring decision, right? These instances are exceptions to the rule, not the norm. To hire smart, be aware you are taking a risk and be willing to suffer the consequences if the hiring decision fails. These situations should be exceptions, not your typical hiring modus operandi.

Using behavior-based interviewing is difficult when you have no past predictors. For example, you might want to hire a person who has never done the task you have in mind. In an instance like this you must call on your creativity. It's easy to ask a seasoned candidate about her experience. It's a lot harder to probe about experiences she does not yet have. Let's look at an example of an interview where the interviewer wants to see if the candidate can learn Microsoft Word (something the candidate has never done):

Interviewer: Tell me about a new task you learned in your current job.
Candidate: When I first started to work at the grocery store, I had to learn how to use the scanning system. It was a real challenge because I'd never done anything like that before, but I finally got the hang of it.
Interviewer: What did you have to do to get the hang of it?
Candidate: For one thing, I had to stick to it. It was frustrating because customers don't understand if you're new and not as fast as someone else.
Interviewer: So sticking to it was one thing you had to do to learn that complicated task. What else did you have to do?
Candidate: I stayed late for several nights to practice when there weren't any customers around. That way I didn't have to deal with people getting upset, which would make me nervous. It really didn't take that long to learn after I did that. After a few times, I got it and felt more confident on the floor.

Notice what this interviewer learned about how this candidate learned new tasks. First, she did not give up even in the face of angry or frustrated customers. Second, she did what it took to learn the task, including staying late to practice on her own. All of the behaviors this candidate shared were based on past experience. The interviewer did not ask: "How do you think you might like to learn Microsoft Word?" In fact, the interviewer need never ask such a question because he found what he needed, namely that the likelihood of this candidate learning the new task was high. The soft skill examined in this behavior-based interview was *ability to learn new tasks*.

Another reason behavior-based interviewing is hard is simply that it takes more forethought and preparation than future-based questions that you can ask any and all candidates. Behavior-based interviewing is based on the candidate's past behavior. Therefore, it is *candidate based*. As you saw in Chapter 1, strategic interviewing is candidate based. Candidate-based interviewing is harder on the interviewer because each interview is different. You can't depend on structured questions or scripted interviewing. Mornell said that with behavior-based interviewing, "You've developed a strategy for which there can be little preparation by the candidate in advance of your meeting."[3] He went on to suggest that a less predictable interview allows the manager to make a better decision on how well a candidate will perform.

Yet managers tend toward structure. They shy away from the effort it takes to interview behaviorally or strategically. ("I don't have time," or "I can tell a good engineer as soon as he walks in the door.") Not until an organization experiences the cost of hiring mistakes do managers recognize the importance interviewing plays in the recruiting process. Unfortunately books that tell you it is easy or, worse, try to give you a formula for interviewing will steer you down a costly, frustrating path. *To hire smart and keep 'em you must have a healthy respect for the interview and take the time to learn how to conduct a strategic interview that employs behavior-based questions.*

In training I tell groups, "As managers you must always be on your toes for the unexpected. Why? Because you're dealing with people." Everything you read and everything you do as a manager teaches you new ideas. You are always adding to your "bag of tricks." Interviewing is no different. It's a management skill that requires constant tweaking, constant work, and adding to that proverbial bag of tricks.

HOW DOES BEHAVIOR-BASED INTERVIEWING FIT WITH THE POINT PROCESS?

Now that you know what behavior-based interviewing is and the importance of formulating your questions around a person's past behavior, let's look at how this kind of interview fits with the POINT process.

Keep in mind that behavior-based interviewing is just one aspect of the POINT process. What behavior-based questioning does is tell you more about how a person might perform in a job. It's a part of the hire-smart strategy. *What it does not do is tell you if the person likes doing the job. It does not answer the second important part of hiring smart, and that's how to keep 'em.*

Furthermore, behavior-based questioning uses only one of the intentional listening skills: probing. And a behavior-based probe is just one kind of probe. As you'll see in Chapter 8, where we will discuss probing in more detail, there are many kinds of probes. Nonetheless, your strategic interview will lead you into a series of probes that include behavior-based probing. Let's illustrate this with an analysis of the example we just looked at.

Interviewer: Tell me about a new task you learned in your current job. (This is not a behavior-based probe but is a perfectly good probe.)

Candidate: When I first started to work at the grocery store, I had to learn how to use the scanning system. It was a real challenge because I'd never done anything like that before, but I finally got the hang of it.

Interviewer: What did you have to do to get the hang of it? (This is a behavior-based probe.)

Candidate: For one thing, I had to stick to it. It was frustrating because customers don't understand if you're new and not as fast as someone else.

Interviewer: So sticking to it was one thing you had to do to learn that complicated task. What else did you have to do? (This is a paraphrase and then a behavior-based probe.)

Candidate: I stayed late for several nights to practice when there weren't any customers around. That way I didn't have to deal with people getting upset, which would make me nervous. It really didn't take that long to learn after I did that. After a few times, I got it and felt more confident on the floor.

In this example the interviewer began with a general probe that led to a series of behavior-based questions. This example represents a typical method for using behavior-based interviewing in the POINT process. The goal is to get to performance, not to interrogate the candidate.

What is a probe? Probes are *open questions* designed to dig deeper for information.

Open versus Closed Questions

An open question is a question that asks for more than a single-word response. It is designed to get the candidate to elaborate on an issue, event or behavior; for example, "How did you decide on banking as a career?"

A closed question is a question that asks the candidate for a one-word or a single-item response; for example, "Did you finish that project?" or "When you attended that seminar, did you go alone or with others?"

Closed questions by their very nature are not probes. This means, if your intention is to dig deeper—that is, to learn more—you must probe with an open question. Nonetheless I hear managers ask closed questions countless times in interviews when they mean to probe. For example, they ask, "Did you find that job hard to do?" or "Do you enjoy your present job?" Both of these closed questions are designed to solicit more information. If the candidate answered with a "yes" or "no," the interviewer would likely not hire her. Nonetheless, the interviewer erred, not the candidate, because she asked a closed question. The interviewer should have asked, "What did you find hard in that job?" or "Tell me what you enjoy doing in your present job." Both of these open probes ask the candidate for more than a yes-or-no answer. Note that you never ask closed probes, but you may at certain strategic times ask closed questions.

Here are some instances when it is appropriate to ask closed questions in an interview:

- When you seek specific information; for example, "What year did you graduate from college?" or "Did you finish your master's degree?"
- When you wish to redirect the interview for deeper probing; for example, "Have you ever worked on a team?" If the résumé gives you no indication

of teamwork and teamwork is a target competency, you'll want to ask this question first. The answer will direct you to your next probe.

• To clarify information. Most paraphrases (another intentional listening skill we will look at in Chapter 8) are closed questions; for example, "So you say you have never worked in a team?" or "From what I hear, you say you've never experienced a conflict situation?" These questions are closed because they are asking for a yes-or-no response in order to gain clarity.

• When the interview is drawing to a close. If you have a talkative candidate and the interview is about to close, you choose to ask a closed question in order to end the interview quickly. Ask, "Do you have any questions for me?" instead of "What questions do you have for me?" The closed question suggests to the candidate you do not have time for too many questions. A sensitive candidate will ask one short question. If the candidate proceeds with a long list of questions, that tells you something about that candidate. (He is insensitive to nonverbal cues). The open question invites the candidate to ask as many questions as he likes.

Behavior-based questions are probes and therefore are open questions. But not all probes are behavior based. One problem I've noticed with the literature on behavior-based interviewing is that the interview becomes a series of probes, some behavior-based, others not, but too much probing closes down the interview. For example:

Interviewer:	What did you find rewarding in your last job? (General probe, not behavior-based)
Candidate:	I enjoyed working with the people in my unit.
Interviewer:	How do you relate to people when you find them enjoyable? (Behavior-based probe)
Candidate:	I tend to laugh a lot and cut up. It brings out the lighter side of me when I like the personalities I'm working with. I found that to be true with the people in my unit.
Interviewer:	What did you do when you worked with someone who wasn't fun to be around? (Behavior-based probe using flipside)
Candidate:	I usually tried to get along with them. Sometimes people just had a bad day. Everyone has a bad day once in a while.
Interviewer:	How did you handle those people having a bad day? (Behavior-based probe)
Candidate:	Sometimes I joked with them. But most of the time I left them alone.
Interviewer:	What did you do when you had to deal with them? (Behavior-based probe)

In looking at this interview, you notice all the probes were open: the interviewer asked questions that did not require a single-word answer. Perhaps you noticed that all but one of the probes were based on the candidate's past behavior. They were not future-based questions.

Imagine yourself the candidate in this interview. How might you have felt? Personally, I'd have felt interrogated. When candidates feel interrogated, they do not open up and tell you something they did not intend to tell you. You are less likely to uncover the truth. *Behavior-based interviewing is one way to probe, but it is just one tool in our arsenal when it comes to strategic interviewing and the POINT process.* POINT consists of six intentional listening skills, and probing is just one of them. Behavior-based interviewing represents a single type of probe. As an interviewer you want to develop your skill with behavior-based interviewing in order to determine a person's ability to perform tasks, but you do not want to rely on it as your only tool.

Evaluating Behavior-based Questions

To help you understand what a behavior-based question looks like, let's examine the questions Mornell listed in his book on hiring smart. Remember Mornell taught us about behavior-based interviewing through his lengthy career as a psychiatrist. I was surprised to see, therefore, that the questions he gave as examples were not always behavior-based questions.

- "If you had a word to describe yourself, what would that be?"
- "What are your major strengths and weaknesses?"
- "When have you failed? Describe the circumstances and how you dealt with and learned from the experience."
- "What is the best job you've had and why?"
- "If you had no economic or practical considerations and you could have any job or jobs you wanted, what would they be and why?"
- "How would you choose to spend additional time if you had it?"[4]

Looking at these questions, can you pick out the one behavior-based question?

If you said, "When have you failed? Describe the circumstances and how you dealt with and learned from the experience," you are correct. This question focuses on the past (times when the candidate failed), and it looks at behavior (how the candidate dealt with those failures). Let's analyze the other questions to understand why they are not behavior-based.

"If you had a word to describe yourself, what would that be?" Behavior-based questions are based on behaviors. What behavior are you looking for

here? The interviewer is asking for a single attribute, not a behavior. Further-more, how does this question describe some behavior in the past? This question is typically used in structured interviews. Not only is it one you could ask of any candidate who walks through the door—a sure test that it is not strategic—but candidates are also prepared to answer this question (remember what Mornell told us about behavior-based questions not being predictable and there-fore better able to ascertain performance). Strategic interviews using POINT are designed to strip away the superficial to uncover a new truth. This question does not do that. If, however, you wish to learn how this candidate sees herself in order to determine how well she reads nonverbal cues (a soft skill), then you might reframe this question as follows: *"Throughout your career, how have you uncovered your personal talents?"*

"What are your major strengths and weaknesses?" Similar to the previous example, structured interviewers typically ask this question, and candidates come with prepared answers. My guess is most of you answered this question in the interviews you've experienced in your career. Recently I heard of an in-stance where an interviewer asked a candidate, "What are your major weak-nesses?" and the candidate answered, "Chocolate chip cookies." His amusing response illustrates what little value this question has.

If, instead, your goal is to determine the candidate's view of himself, you'll need to ask a series of questions, such as:

Interviewer: Describe how you responded to your last performance evaluation. (Behavior-based probe)
Candidate: I was pleased because my boss noted things about my work that I was proud of.
Interviewer: What kinds of things were you proud of? (General probe)
Candidate: I was proud of getting good test results on a product we have been trying to bring to the market. I was proud because I had to persist when others might have given up, and then I had to use some different approaches. But we finally got there.
Interviewer: So you were proud of your ability to persist and be creative on tough projects? (Paraphrase)
Candidate: Yes. I was also proud that my boss noted those traits.
Interviewer: What other strengths did your boss note? (General probe)

Once this interviewer revealed all the strengths this person saw in himself based on his performance reviews, she might address weaknesses in a simi-lar fashion by asking, "What things in your last performance review troubled you?" The combined tools—probes and paraphrases—give the interview more flexibility to keep the candidate talking in a nonthreatening environment.

A series of strategic questions takes more time than a structured interview where the interviewer asks one question. But the information you uncover more than justifies the time it takes.

"What is the best job you've had and why?" What is behavior-based about this question? Again, we cannot envision a behavior in the past. Although not behavior-based, this is a general probe and definitely one you may want to ask in a strategic interview.

As you saw in Chapter 2, strategic interviews have a dual purpose: ascertaining performance capability and staying power. As interviewers, therefore, you are interested in both whether the person can perform the job and whether he enjoys doing it. Maybe this candidate can do the job, but if he is unhappy, he will look elsewhere. We aim to hire smart and keep 'em. This question illustrates where behavior-based questioning helps us uncover one aspect of the POINT process but not the other. Let's look at how an interview might go if we reword the question for a more strategic aim, using behavior-based questions:

Interviewer:	Tell me what you liked doing in your last job. (Behavior-based probe)
Candidate:	I love working with people. When I got a chance to help someone use the website and achieve success, it really felt good.
Interviewer:	How did you help people use the website? (Behavior-based probe)
Candidate:	I would spend time with them and guide them through, usually on the telephone. The key is not to get frustrated. Usually they got frustrated when they couldn't understand what I wanted them to do. So I'd calm them down, and we'd approach the problem another way. That was fun because I could feel the person respond. They'd say things like, "Oh, yes, now I see." Things like that.
Interviewer:	So you enjoyed experiencing success when people understood how to use the site. (Summary to identify what the candidate enjoyed)
Candidate:	Yes, and they'd always be so grateful.
Interviewer:	What else did you enjoy about your last job? (General probe)

This interview looks at past experiences, but the goal is not so much to determine what the candidate did (behavior) as to determine satisfaction. The interviewer learned that this candidate likes feeling success when helping others. If the job has those kinds of opportunities in it, this candidate might be a good fit.

BEHAVIOR-BASED VERSUS FUTURE-BASED QUESTIONS

Before we look at Mornell's last two questions, let's define the difference between behavior-based and future-based questions. We know that behavior-based questions are predicated on past behavior. Future-based questions, on the other hand, ask candidates to speculate. They look into the future.

To interview smart, you must avoid future-based questions. Why? To answer that question, let's look at an example.

Interviewer:	If you had two employees who both performed well in their jobs but could not get along no matter what you tried to do, how would you handle the situation? (Future-based probe)
Candidate:	I would sit both employees down and tell them that they must get along or they would both have to leave.
Interviewer:	So you'd risk losing two good employees? (Reality test)
Candidate:	If that's what it takes. Otherwise morale in the department might go down. But if I make it clear that they both must work together to keep their jobs, my guess is they'll work out their differences.

Whether or not the interviewer liked this answer makes little difference. You still do not know what this employee would actually do in a real situation. That's the rub with all future-based questions. Again, candidates strive to answer questions the way they think the interviewer wants them answered. Future-based questions tell us nothing about a person's performance now or in the future.

Let's look at the last two questions Mornell presented as behavior-based examples:

- "If you had no economic or practical considerations and you could have any job or jobs you wanted, what would they be and why?"
- "How would you choose to spend additional time if you had it?"

Both of these questions ask the candidate to speculate. In the first one the candidate must respond to a question that in the real world would never happen. This kind of speculation into the future, especially an unrealistic future, is neither behavior based nor strategic. If the interviewer is trying to get at job satisfaction, why not simply ask, "Tell me what you enjoy doing in your current job?"

The second question also asks the candidate to hypothesize. Clearly the interviewer wants to learn what the candidate enjoys doing when she's not working. Again, why not simply ask, "Tell me what you like to do when you're not at work?"

One future-based question that comes up in nearly every interview is, "What do you want to do in five years?" This question has a number of flaws.

First, it asks the candidate to speculate, and second, it is a question all candidates anticipate.

In asking this question an interviewer might wish to know either how the candidate goes about setting goals or how ambitious the candidate is. Let's examine two behavior-based questions with these targets:

"Tell me what you've done to advance your career to this point?" This question begins to uncover the candidate's ambition and requires that the candidate give specific behavioral examples to respond.

"What goals did you set for yourself to get to your current professional level?" Here, the interviewer is specifically looking at goal-setting, and again the candidate must give specific behavioral examples to respond.

HOW TO ASK BEHAVIOR-BASED QUESTIONS
WITH INEXPERIENCED CANDIDATES

Many managers hire people right out of high school, vocational school, or college. In those instances candidates are young and their experiences limited. How can you still keep a focus on past behavior?

As we noted earlier in this chapter, *when candidates have little or no experience, the interview becomes more difficult.* This statement often surprises managers because they believe that their most difficult interviews are with seasoned professionals. In fact, those of you who hire for the very basic jobs—production employees, stylists, bookkeepers, receptionists, sales clerks, cooks, waiters, busboys—face the most challenging interviews. Many of you, who deal with these kinds of interviews, probably experience high levels of turnover. One way to reduce that turnover is to interview smarter. But how can you do that when your candidates often tell you nothing and their experience is limited? Before we look at some ways you can interview these candidates, let's revisit your recruiting process.

If you hire hair dressers, for example, where have you found your most successful employees? Was it at the local vocational school? Perhaps an instructor in that school can help you locate candidates. Was it from referrals from other employees? If you simply place an ad in the local paper and expect the best candidates to walk through the door, you may be disappointed. You must do some research to uncover where the best candidates are and then go after them. That's why the process is called *recruiting*. The word means actively finding people to fill your jobs. *Help Wanted* on the door may not be enough.

Who interviews your candidates? When we look at the O in the POINT process (Chapter 6), you'll learn the importance of openness in the interview. You'll discover how to create trust. When management-level people interview low-level people, trust suffers. Imagine if you were a high school graduate looking for a job as a cashier, and your boss interviewed you. How much would you tell that manager? If, on the other hand, another cashier, who had been on the job and successful for a period of time, interviewed you, how much might you reveal? *The more alike we are to the person sitting across from us, the greater the chance for trust to happen.* This does not mean that the managers do not interview for lower-paid jobs. It does mean that added to the mix of people interviewing are people in similar positions.

Take a look at the case example that illustrates how to interview people who do not have a lot of experience.

Change Future-Based Questions into Behavior-Based Questions

- If in five years you were offered my job, what would you have to do now to reach that place? *Five years ago you worked as a pharmacy consultant. What did you have to do in those five years to reach your current professional level?*
- What are your future educational plans? *What factors motivated you to complete your undergraduate degree?*
- If you supervised ten people and five of them left in the last year, what would you need to do? *How have you handled turnover in your previous jobs?*
- How can you maintain good morale in this difficult economic environment? *In this difficult economic environment, give me an example of something you have done to keep morale high among your staff.*

Notice there is a wide array of behavior-based questions you might create in these situations, but all of them must focus on the past and look for specific behaviors. Often the first question you ask isn't enough to get at what you're looking for. You must follow up with additional questions that dig deeper and strip away further until you have enough information to determine if the person can perform the job.

In this chapter we explored behavior-based interviewing. We learned that when you focus on a person's past behavior you have a better chance of determining future performance. Of course, there is no guarantee. What you want to do in the interview is increase your chance to hire smart. Behavior-based interviewing combined with the POINT process will do that.

We also learned in this chapter that relying on behavior-based interviewing alone will not lead you to smart interviewing. Instead, behavior-based interviews are one more item to add to your bag of tricks to enable you to hire smart and keep 'em. Another way to increase your hiring success is through team interviews. Chapter 4 will look at the value of the team interview, namely what works and what doesn't work when performing team interviews. We will also give you tips on how to hire smart with teams.

CASE: HOW TO INTERVIEW PEOPLE
WITH LIMITED EXPERIENCE

The candidate is applying for a cashier position in a local grocery. The candidate has a high school degree and no experience.

After a brief icebreaker, the interviewer asks:

Interviewer: *What were your favorite courses in school?* (general probe)

Candidate: *I enjoyed shop and physical education.*

Interviewer: *What did you enjoy about shop?* (general probe)

Candidate: *I liked to make things with my hands.*

Interviewer: *I used to like making things, too. What kinds of things did you make?* (behavior-based probe)

Candidate: *We had a lot of projects. Sometimes we even made shelves out of wood. That was fun. Once we made a drawer for a desk. We had to take the measurements and everything. It was hard, but I felt good when we did it.*

Interviewer: *When you say "we" did it, did you work on that project with others?* (closed question for specific information)

Candidate: *Yeah, a group of three of us worked together, taking measurements and figuring out what to do, and the teacher helped, too.*

Interviewer: *Sometimes it's hard to work with other people. How was that for you?* (general probe)

Candidate: *It was fun.*

Interviewer: *So you like working with others?* (paraphrase)

Candidate: *I do because sometimes somebody has an idea you didn't have.*

Interviewer: *What about PE? What did you like about that?* (general probe)

Candidate: *I like being active.*

Interviewer: *What particular sports did you enjoy the most?* (general probe)

Candidate: *I really liked basketball. I'm not very tall, but I'm fast. I played guard a lot, and that was fun.*

Interviewer: *How was it playing with other people?* (general probe)

Candidate: *I had lots of friends. Sometimes we played on the same team, and sometimes we played against each other.*

Interviewer: *It must have felt uncomfortable playing against friends.* (reflection)

Candidate: *Not really. We all did it.*

Interviewer: *How did you manage to keep your friends after you beat them in a game?* (behavior-based probe)

Candidate: *We used to go out together to the movies or something afterward. Once I had a friend who played kinda rough. He was mad at the end of the game and stomped off the court. I told him to chill. He settled down. Sometimes they just need to go off by themselves for a while, and then they're fine.*

ANALYSIS OF INTERVIEW

The interviewer asked just two behavior-based questions but many general probes. The first question, "What were your favorite courses in school?" asked the candidate to reflect back on past courses he enjoyed. Here the interviewer was not looking at behavior but at enjoyment. Often you need to soften the first question in any interview, particularly with a candidate where trust factors might be an issue. This question enabled the candidate to talk about something he knew and to do so from the vantage point of the past.

Later the interviewer asked him about the kinds of things he built in shop as well as the way he did it. She asked him about the sports he played and the way he interacted with his teammates. Several times the interviewer used intentional listening skills that were not probes in order to prevent the interview from becoming threatening. ("So you like working with others" and "It must have felt uncomfortable playing against friends."). In one instance the interviewer asked a closed question to redirect the interview: "When you say 'we,' did that mean you worked with others?"

From this brief snapshot of an interview, let's determine what we learned about this candidate:

- The candidate enjoys working with others.
- The candidate likes to make new things.
- The candidate likes to use his hands.
- The candidate is sensitive to others.
- The candidate enjoys competition but doesn't lose friends over it.

Would this candidate make a good cashier in the grocery store? To answer that question we must know what target competencies the interviewer was addressing. If working with people and being able to learn new things that require manual dexterity are competencies for a cashier, the answer would likely be yes, this candidate is a good fit.

PRACTICE EXERCISE

Pick out the behavior-based questions.

1. Give me an example of when you had to handle a conflict situation.
2. If you had to make a decision where one choice would be of value to the company but more work for your staff and the other would value staff but hurt the company in the long run, what would you do?
3. How would you handle an ethical situation where you knew your boss did something unprofessional?
4. What did you enjoy most in your previous job?
5. What made you decide to apply with us for a new position?
6. How have you dealt with conflict in teams in your recent jobs?
7. What are your greatest strengths?
8. Imagine it is five years from now; where do you see yourself professionally?
9. What criteria did you use to accept the offer from your last job?
10. When two people disagree, it's usually a personality conflict. How have you handled personality conflicts in the past?

See Appendix A for answers.

FOUR

The Power of Team Interviews

In Chapter 3 we looked at behavior-based interviewing as a method for hiring smarter. We now understand that as interviewers we must be focused on the candidate with an eye on past behavior. It takes enormous energy to do that. Interviewers must be on their toes every second to hear what the candidates are saying and not saying through their verbal and nonverbal cues. In addition, interviewers must think about their strategy. Team interviews relieve some of the pressure. Having another person there enables the interviewer to relax, knowing that if he misses something, his partner will see it.

Team interviews can be very powerful, or they can fail miserably. To hire smart, you want to increase the odds for successful team interviews. In this chapter we'll look at what makes team interviews powerful as well as the pros and cons for team interviewing. We'll also give you tips for how to interview effectively with a partner, and we will illustrate all this with team interview examples. Finally we'll help you become a better team player by understanding the power of groupthink and team dynamics.

WHAT IS A TEAM INTERVIEW?

A team interview is any interview involving two or more interviewers and one candidate. For our purposes we will include panel interviews (three or more interviewers) in this definition. Whenever we discuss team interviews, you can apply the same principles to panels. But keep in mind that *the most effective team interview consists of no more than two interviewers.* More than two people can intimidate the candidate and thereby threaten the openness in the interview. We'll talk more about openness in Chapter 6.

Some organizations use a combination of interview types in their process, namely two-person interviews, panels, and solo interviews. As you construct your process, you must determine what you're trying to accomplish in order to identify what type of interview to select. In this chapter we'll explore the two-on-one interview to enable you to add that to your mix.

WHAT DOES AN EFFECTIVE TEAM INTERVIEW LOOK LIKE?

- Two interviewers balance one another. One may be new to the organization; the other may be a more seasoned employee. One may be a production associate while the other works in management. One may be an engineer, and the other may be a human resources associate. One may be an administrator, the other a practitioner. You wouldn't pair together two vice presidents or the president and vice president, just as you wouldn't pair two line workers. You strive for a balanced team.

- Each interviewer brings a different focus to the team interview, and both are equal regardless of their job titles. If a vice president partners with an administrative associate, both show equal respect for the other's knowledge and skill. If one interviewer is new to the organization and the other seasoned, the seasoned interviewer does not dominate. You must never downplay (either verbally or nonverbally) the knowledge of your interview partner.

- When the interview begins, each interviewer introduces herself rather than one interviewer introducing both. For example: "My name is Larry Smith, and I'm a photographer with the company." "My name is Mary Jones, and I'm the human resources manager. We are here today . . . " rather than, "My name is Larry Smith. I'm a photographer for the company, and this is Mary Smith. She works in human resources." In the first instance the candidate gets the impression that neither interviewer is more important than the other. If one person introduces both, the candidate assumes that the person making the introductions carries more weight.

- Although the interview is well planned, it appears conversational. One interviewer asks a question; the other may follow up or tag with another question. The interviewers pause after each statement in order to allow the other interviewer to chime in. It's perfectly appropriate for one partner to ask of the other, "Do you have anything to add?" If, on the other hand, one interviewer exhausts her questions before the other says one word, and the other does the same, there's no point in the team interview.

- Both interviewers plan the interview strategy together. Joint planning enables both to know what each is driving at. During the interview, however, both respond to the candidate with flexibility. Knowing the overall plan keeps the interviewers on a clear path but allows for diversions.

PROS AND CONS FOR TEAM INTERVIEWS

Team interviews are not the be-all, end-all to interviewing. As we said in the introduction to this book, no magic formula exists to enable you to hire smart and keep 'em. Interviewing is much too complex for that. To hire smart, however, you look for ways to increase the odds of making a good hiring decision. Team interviews provide one way to accomplish that goal. They offer a good option in certain situations, particularly when your organization has many people interviewing every candidate. If you are a small operation, team interviews may not work for you.

Pros for Team Interviews

- Two interviewers bring a broader perspective to the interview process. Your partner's knowledge and experience enable her to see something you might miss. This is particularly true when you pair a technical person with a human resource person. Each brings different knowledge and skill to the interview table.

- The candidate may feel more rapport with one interviewer than another. Team interviews increase the likelihood for a candidate to open up and share something he didn't intend to share. In other words, team interviews offer the potential for "good cop, bad cop," except in an interview there are no "bad" cops—just one interviewer liked a little more than the other. As you'll see in Chapter 6 when we look at openness in the interview, there is rarely a time when an interviewer intentionally intimidates a candidate.

- Two people limit the influence of biases and perceptions (see Chapter 1) and give us more filters. If you get zapped by a perception, perhaps your partner did not.

- Two interviewers working together in the résumé planning phases of POINT spin ideas off each other and do a more thorough job than one person working alone. Often your partner sees something on the résumé that you do not see. She wishes to explore an angle that may not have occurred to you.

- What one interviewer misses in a strategic interview, the other catches. As we've said, strategic interviewing requires you to listen with your full antenna on high alert. No matter how hard you try, you'll miss something. Two interviewers are less likely to allow an important piece of information (including a nonverbal cue) to slip by. For example, suppose your partner asks a candidate what he finds troubling about working in teams and the candidate's eyes dart before saying, "Teams are great fun to work with. I love their creativity and bouncing ideas off other people. So, I guess I can't think of anything that troubles me about working on teams." Your partner responds, "So it sounds as if you love working with teams." Clearly your partner missed the nonverbal cue—eyes darting. You might follow up with something like, "Let me see if I'm clear. You've never had a situation with a team where members did not perform as you'd hoped or members got in each other's way?" What you've done here is help your partner catch a nonverbal cue.

- Two interviewers represent a cross section of the organization and thereby give the candidate a broader picture of the company. You need not say to the candidate that your organization consists of administrators and clinicians; the candidate knows that as soon as you introduce yourselves. As the two interviewers sprinkle in information about the organization throughout the interview and share their views from different perspectives, the candidate gleans a wider picture of the company.

- Team interviewing shows the candidate that teams and teamwork are important values in the organization. Again, you need not tell the candidate that your company believes in teamwork. The candidate sees teamwork in action during the interview.

- Team interviews help to protect the interviewers from legal allegations. As you will see in Chapter 5, interviews provide a high-risk place for litigation. When you interview as a team, you protect one another from unfounded allegations. Furthermore, if you slip on a touchy legal question, your partner can rescue you and vice versa.

Cons for Team Interviews

- Two interviewers to one candidate can intimidate the candidate and cause the candidate to shut down. This is especially true for lower-level positions where candidates have less sophisticated communication skills. If you decide to use team interviews to interview hourly employees, be sure to include hourly employees as interviewers.

- When one of the two interviewers takes over and controls the interview, it becomes uncomfortable for the candidate and the partner interviewer.

- Team interviews take more time than solo interviews. A solo interview often takes 30 to 45 minutes. Team interviews can last as long as 90 minutes.

- With three people in the interview room and two of them interviewers, the candidate may not have as much opportunity to talk. One aim of the interview is to get the candidate to talk at least 75 percent of the time. For a team interview that goal becomes more challenging. What this means is if you are one of the interviewers, you can only consume approximately 12.5 percent of the talk time. If your partner is chatty, this might present a problem.

- If the interviewers have not prepared adequately, they may not give the candidate sufficient time to respond. In one-on-one communication, a split second elapses when a candidate finishes talking before the interviewer asks the next question. In a team interview, if your partner jumps in with the next question, that split second is lost. Candidates feel they do not have a chance to finish a response before the next question comes at them. It feels like shot-gun questioning.

A TEAM INTERVIEW CASE EXAMPLE THAT WENT WRONG

Interviewer 1:   My name is Martha Williams and I'm a social worker for this agency. My job is to help children connect with the right families. It's not easy sometimes because it's hard not to get too attached to the child. I had to learn that early on.

Interviewer 2:   (jumps in) My name is Robert Lewis, and I am a social worker as well. It's a great job. You'll see if we hire you how rewarding it is. Some days I go home and really feel as if I've made a difference in someone's life. You can't get that with any other job. And believe me, I know because I've done many other things, even selling cars. Today, I am going to ask you some questions, and Martha will ask you some as well. At the end of the interview you can jump in with all your questions, and then we'll take you on a brief tour of the facility.

We should have you out of here in a couple of hours. How does that sound to you?

Candidate: It sounds fine.

Robert: Good, so I see on your résumé that you got your degree in finance before going back for your master's in social work. I did a similar thing when I was in school, majoring in computer science and then switching to social work. What made you decide to change fields?

Candidate: I wanted to do more than deal with numbers all day. I had been doing that long enough. (Notice the ratio of candidate speaking to interviewer speaking. If you had to divide it up, what percentage would you give the interviewer talk time versus the candidate talk time?)

Robert: But it seems a big jump from finance to social work. Couldn't you have gone into marketing or some other business-related field?

Candidate: I wasn't interested in marketing. Actually I had always been interested in social work, but my parents encouraged me to major in finance.

Robert: Yeah, parents can have their ideas for what we ought to do. My parents wanted me to study law. I never could get

Candidate:	interested in it no matter how I tried. How about that first job? Tell me what made you leave after just six months. Jones Incorporated was a very small company that had been in business for only a couple of years. They overextended when they hired me. Unfortunately they didn't generate enough money to keep me on the payroll. They gave me a good reference, and I had no trouble landing the next job with Wilkins.
Robert:	That must have been a real blow and a shock to lose your first job like that.
Candidate:	It was hard, but they were so nice to me. They helped me find the job at Wilkins. I couldn't fault them.
Martha:	You managed to keep that job at Wilkins for a long time, and I see you moved up in the company. Tell me what you liked about working there.
Candidate:	I really enjoyed the people. Once I had a few people to supervise, I enjoyed the challenge of helping people do their job. Together we reached goals I wouldn't have imagined.
Robert:	How did you manage to get people to reach those high goals?

Interview Analysis

The candidate talked very little at the beginning of the interview. Both interviewers talked a lot without giving the candidate an opportunity to speak until he said, "It sounds fine." Early in any interview, the talk ratio of interviewer to candidate will be more interviewer heavy than later into the interview. In other words, right off the bat we won't have the 75:25 ratio, but it should be at least 50:50. In this case it was probably more like the interviewers talking 90 percent and the candidate 10 percent. Notice, however, the candidate does speak up more as the interview progresses.

Another place where this team interview faltered is that both interviewers represented the same kind of job. That may be fine if one of them had been on the job a long time and the other was relatively new. But neither indicated the length of service.

Before we look at how Robert failed as an interview partner, let's examine where he got high marks.

- He explained the process to the candidate, namely that the interviewers would ask him questions, then he could ask his questions, and afterward they would take him on a tour.

- He shared a little information about himself before asking the candidate the first questions: "I did a similar thing when I was in school, majoring in computer science and then switching to social work. What made you decide to change fields?" This was a good way to break the ice.

- He asked good open questions; for example, "How about that first job? Tell me what made you leave after just six months."
- He did not simply use probes. He used other intentional listening skills as well; for example, "That must have been a real blow and a shock to lose your first job like that." This illustrates *reflecting*. Using it here in the interview helped him develop rapport with the candidate.

Robert did a nice job as a solo interviewer, but he made some critical mistakes as a team interviewer. Let's examine how he blew the team interview.

- He talked too long in his introduction. It was okay for him to lead with the first question and to share the process, but he gave too much information at the outset. You do want to sprinkle a little information about yourself at the beginning, but Robert did too much of that in two places: first, when he said, "Some days I go home and really feel as if I've made a difference in someone's life. You can't get that with any other job. And believe me, I know because I've done many other things, even selling cars," and later when he said, "Yeah, parents can have their ideas for what we ought to do. My parents wanted me to study law. I never could get interested in it no matter how much I tried."
- He took over the interview. Once Martha introduced herself, she did not have another opportunity to speak until much later. By time she spoke, Robert had created rapport with the candidate, and the candidate probably wondered why Martha was there.
- To make matters worse, Robert jumped in again after Martha had a chance to finally ask a question. He totally dominated the interview.

ROBERT AND MARTHA'S TEAM INTERVIEW, TAKE TWO

Interviewer 1:   My name is Martha Roberts, and I'm a social worker for this agency. My job is to help children connect with the right families. I've been with the company for just under a year.

Interviewer 2:   (jumps in) My name is Robert Lewis, and I am a social worker as well, but I've been around longer than Martha. I started here 15 years ago. Between the two of us, you'll get a good idea of how our company operates. How does that sound to you, Jamie?

Candidate: Great. I'm looking forward to it.

Martha: Today our plan is to ask you some questions about yourself and to allow you to ask us some questions.
At the end of the interview, we'll take you on a brief tour of the facility. We should have you out of here
in a couple of hours. I hope that meets with your schedule.

Candidate: My flight doesn't leave until tonight. Thanks.

Robert: Good. So I see on your résumé that you got your degree in finance before going back for your master's in social work. I did a similar thing when I was in school, majoring in computer science and then switching to social work. What made you decide to change fields?

Candidate: I wanted to do more than deal with numbers all day. I had been doing that long enough.

Martha: What did you find troubling about dealing with numbers?

Candidate: Oh, I don't mind numbers that much. It's just boring to deal with them all day long. I'm much happier dealing with more challenges, and I find people very challenging.

Robert: So you didn't like dealing with numbers, but wasn't it a big jump from finance to social work?

Candidate: Actually I had always been interested in social work, but my parents encouraged me to major in finance. My dad thought I'd make more money in that field. I don't mind finance, and I did well in the courses in college, but when I started working, I realized I was disillusioned.

Martha: Jamie, let's go back a minute. Tell me more about what you find challenging about dealing with people.

Candidate: People come to you with all kinds of issues that must be dealt with. I worked as a sales clerk in a very busy store in high school. I loved having the satisfaction that I helped someone solve a problem or find the perfect item. That was one reason I was interested in social work. Another was I had an uncle who was a social worker. He talked about some of his clients and what he was able to do for them. It fascinated me. Just thinking about that kind of job excites me. Working in finance didn't do that.

Martha: It sounds as though you are very excited to be making this career change.

Candidate: I really am. It's something I've dreamed of for a long time.

Robert: How about that first job? Tell me what made you leave after just six months.

Candidate: Jones Incorporated was a very small company that had only been in business for a couple of years. They overextended when they hired me. Unfortunately they didn't generate enough money to keep me on the payroll. They gave me a good reference, and I had no trouble landing the next job with Wilkins.

Robert: That must have been a real blow and a shock to lose your first job like that.

Candidate: It was hard, but they were so nice to me. They helped me find the job at Wilkins. I couldn't fault them.

Martha: You managed to keep that job at Wilkins for a long time, and I see you moved up in the company. Tell me what you liked about working there.

Analysis of Robert and Martha Interview, Take Two

- Both Martha and Robert asked questions equally; neither dominated the interview.
- The candidate spoke more. You want to avoid asking a hard question that will force the candidate to speak a lot early in the interview, but you do want him to speak as much as he wishes. Jamie started out slowly, which is common, but he picked up quickly into the interview.
- Both interviewers created rapport with the candidate. You want the interview to feel as if you are having a conversation with three people, not an interrogation by a panel. Robert still sprinkled in information about himself, but not as much as in the first example.
- The interviewers, although both social workers, told Jamie that one was a relatively new hire and the other a seasoned hire.

The second interview with Jamie felt more like a team interview. Often people new to team interviewing make the mistake Robert made in the first instance because they have interviewed solo for most of their careers. It's hard to break old habits.

Let's examine another interview. This time the interviewers are not from a similar part of the company but represent different branches. When you conduct a team interview with people from different parts of the company, you have an opportunity to focus questions related to your area of interest.

TEAM INTERVIEW WITH PATRICK AND LUCY

Patrick: Good morning, I'm Patrick Hayes. I am a shift supervisor with our company.

Lucy: I'm Lucy Cobb. I work in human resources. We're going to ask you a few questions just to get to know you. May we call you Mary?

Mary:	Absolutely.
Patrick:	Great, Mary. So how do you like living in Blacksburg?
Candidate:	It's okay, but the town is one of the reasons I want to leave. I've lived in Blacksburg for almost three years. The town is really drying up. There wasn't much here three years ago, but since the Ford plant closed, the place is really dead.
Lucy:	You say the community is one reason you want to leave; what other reasons are driving you from your present job?
Candidate:	There are things I really like about my work. I love working independently and being creative. My boss gives me lots of leeway. That's how I've been able to go back to school. But I've gone about as far as I can go in this job. There's no room for advancement in the company, and there's really nothing else available in the community.
Lucy:	I had a similar situation early in my career. That's one reason I moved to human resources. What sorts of career paths are you looking for?
Candidate:	I'm currently studying industrial engineering at school. During the last two years, I took courses at the community college. Then last year I returned to Wofford full time so I could find a job in my field.
Patrick:	By "in your field," what do you mean?
Candidate:	I know I won't be able to make as much money as I do in my current job because beginning positions in engineering start out at less. But I'm willing to take a cut to get into engineering.
Lucy:	So you're saying you don't mind making less money to change career paths?
Candidate:	That's right.
Patrick:	Mary, tell me about the courses you've taken at Wofford.
Candidate:	Since I'd been out of school for a few years, I took courses at the community college first on analysis of technical data, project planning, and control. Once I got to Wofford, I took a lot of computer courses to bring me up to speed on the software currently used by industrial engineers.
Patrick:	What computer courses did you take?
Candidate:	I took an introduction to C programming, a course on computer-aided design, two on WordPerfect, and one on Microsoft Word.
Patrick:	What languages do you feel proficient in?
Candidate:	WordPerfect, Microsoft Word, Lotus, QI-Analyst, SIMAN.
Lucy:	Mary, you said you liked the creativity and working independently in your current job. Describe a situation for me

when you had independence and the opportunity to be creative in your work.

Analysis of Interview with Lucy and Patrick

- Notice how quickly the interviewers got Mary talking. After a very brief introduction, they asked her a general open question.

- Lucy dealt with general areas of interest, career path, location desire, and job satisfaction while Patrick dealt with more technical issues like courses taken and computer language proficiency.

- Lucy sprinkled a little information about herself in the interview when she said, "I had a similar situation early in my career. That's one reason I moved to human resources." This technique helped build rapport with the candidate without dominating the interview.

- Right after Lucy had asked several questions related to topics of interest to her, Patrick jumped in with, "By 'in your field,' what do you mean?" He did not deviate too far from Lucy's line of questioning, but he entered the fray. Team interviews do not have to be back-and-forth like a tennis match. Instead they flow in a natural progression. Patrick waited until just the right moment to come in. Had he waited longer, he would have lost the opportunity. If your partner tends to wait too long to jump in, you can say something like: "Patrick, didn't you have a situation like Mary's when you first started working here?"

- The interviewers used two intentional listening skills, probing and paraphrasing. By throwing in a paraphrase, they kept the interview from getting too threatening. Patrick did not have as much rapport with the candidate. Two things he might have done to get closer to the candidate are (1) refrain from so many probes—he probed every time; and (2) sprinkle some information about himself, something technical people find hard to do but important nonetheless.

- The last question Lucy asked illustrates a well-designed behavior-based question: "Describe a situation for me when you had independence and the opportunity to be creative in your work." This question went back to the candidate's disclosure in the beginning that she liked working independently and being creative.

THE IMPACT OF GROUPTHINK ON TEAM INTERVIEWS

Groupthink is a sociological phenomenon that was defined in the 1960s after the Bay of Pigs incident. Put simply it means *everyone decides to do something stupid together*. It affects groups when perceptions take over and control a group decision. For example, if someone walks into a group meeting and says,

"We all know who the best candidate is, so let's get on with this decision and get back to work." That someone might be the president of the company or someone of equally high stature in the organization. Once a statement like this is made, people often shut down and keep their doubts to themselves.

According to Whyte, this is essentially what happened to President John Kennedy in 1961.[1] Shortly after Kennedy became president, he faced the decision of whether or not to invade Cuba. The previous administration had hatched the idea to launch a preemptive strike on the island. Kennedy, being new and not having been privy to previous discussions about the plan, wondered if such action was in the best interests of the United States. He consulted with his key national advisors, both in group settings and individually. All the advisors wanted to do what everyone else wanted to do. No one wanted to criticize the previous administration or to appear to oppose an idea pushed by the military. Even though many people had doubts, they did not voice their concerns; they did not wish to "rock the boat." Instead of sharing their unease about the outcome of such an invasion, they agreed to the operation known as the Bay of Pigs. Today, in hindsight, we know that operation failed. President Kennedy learned an important lesson and did not repeat his mistake during the Cuban Missile Crisis. From that point forward he made sure people felt safe enough to voice their doubts.

Groupthink is a very common phenomenon but can lead to dangerous hiring mistakes if interviewers are not careful. People credit Alfred Sloan, long-time CEO of General Motors, with saying, "If all my top people agree to do something, I send them home to sleep on it. I never proceed when everyone agrees." I don't know if Sloan actually said this, but what he was talking about was the power of the groupthink phenomenon long before the term was ever coined.

To understand groupthink you must understand group dynamics. In the mid-1960s, Bruce Tuckman studied the way teams work and noticed emerging patterns.[2] These patterns became the crux of today's understanding of group dynamics. Tuckman demonstrated that all teams go through certain stages of growth and that within those stages certain things happen uniformly even though each team differs because each team is made up of different individuals. In other words, *groups of people act in similar ways when they become a part of a team*. Because two or more people comprise a team, you and your interview partner are potentially subject to groupthink. Knowledge of Tuckman's stages of team development can minimize frustration when working with teams as well as keep groupthink in check.

Tuckman's Stages of Team Development

Tuckman did not actually name the stages that follow. He described them, and the names evolved.

1. *Forming.* When groups come together for the first time, they have little knowledge of each other. Even though members want to be part of the team, they also pull away. Their desire to be part of the team typifies our human desire for belonging. At the same time individuals fear they will lose their individuality. For that reason some people call this stage approach/avoidance. The task a team at the forming stage can perform adequately is *orientation* to each other and to the mission of the team.[3] In an interview environment the forming stage begins as soon as the two interviewers sit down to review the résumé. In that initial meeting they must take time to orient to each other before diving into the task. If the two interviewers have worked together before, they should take a few minutes to evaluate how that experience went for them; that is, each partner gives feedback to the other. Also, bear in mind that when the group invites the candidate into the room for the interview, the team returns to the forming stage because the team has added a new member to the mix. That is why it is important to begin the interview with some orientation information as we saw in the interview with Martha and Robert.

2. *Storming.* Tuckman described the second stage of team development as one of the most uncomfortable for any team. In this stage, members recognize the value of the team itself, but they also want the other members to notice and respect their own *individual* worth. Imagine everyone on the team vying for attention. It's the "me-me" stage of group dynamics. Many of you have been in meetings or parts of teams in this stage. You've seen others dominate the group by talking about themselves and their experiences and ignoring others. The only task teams can adequately perform at this stage is *organization* of the conflicting struggles around the team goals.[4] In the interview environment, the storming stage can cause a team interview to break down completely. If one member dominates or struggles against the partner, they find out nothing about the candidate. Usually when one member dominates, the other member pulls away. We saw this happen in the first interview with Martha and Robert. At times, you will face a candidate who attempts to take over the interview. The candidate pontificates about her successes or about her experiences without allowing the interviewers to ask questions. When this happens, the interviewers should not jump in with their own credentials. Instead they should listen and, when the opportunity arises, ask questions that lead to the interview goals but do not threaten the candidate. When people dominate, it often means they feel insecure.

3. *Norming.* After the storming stage, the third stage of team development feels very comfortable to team members, but it can also be one of the most dangerous stages in the process. The norming stage is where

groupthink happens. Members support each other in everything. They acknowledge one another with statements like, "That's a great suggestion," or, "I really like what you are saying." Maintaining group intimacy becomes the motivation of the team.[5] In the norming stage, groups are not yet ready to make decisions. Instead they are quite adept at *data flow*, or open sharing without evaluation. In this stage groups generate creative ideas.

In an interview, whenever you have doubts but are unwilling to share those doubts, ask yourself, "Are we experiencing groupthink?" One of the pros for team interviewing is that you have a little more protection from perceptions: if you got zapped, perhaps your partner did not. What if you both got zapped? Such instances may be the result of groupthink; that is, your partner seems so high on a candidate that you are reluctant to voice your concerns. In those instances, whether it is with you and your partner or with a team of colleagues making a hiring decision, you must become the Alfred Sloan of the group. You must point out that the group is in the norming stage and should wait until members can discuss both the positives and the negatives before making a hiring decision. *Remember no one is perfect. If you can't see any negatives, you may have been zapped by a perception or, worse still, influenced by groupthink.*

4. *Performing*. The fourth stage happens when the group members recognize each other's strengths and weaknesses. Each person willingly listens to one another with a new kind of respect. In the performing stage the group has reached interdependence—I need you and you need me. The ability to share strengths and weaknesses leads the group to its most important task, namely *decision making*. Members finally reach the high-performing stage where they can make decisions in a different way—through the eyes of the team—rather than through the eyes of individuals.[6] Knowing that no team interview begins at the performing stage because the candidate pushes the team back to the forming stage as soon as she walks through the door, we can still gain the value of teams when we understand the dynamics of groups and work within that framework. This is the ultimate goal of your interviewing team. If your find yourself feeling comfortable in your team and notice team members laughing together and teasing one another, you are likely in the performing stage.

5. *Adjourning*. Tuckman's final stage of team development occurs after team members finish their task and are ready to evaluate their work. Team interviewers do this at the end of each interview. The ultimate task in the adjourning stage is *evaluation*. Chapter 10 will take us through that process. You'll see that interviewers do not simply

evaluate the candidate in this final stage. They evaluate the team's success: How did we do as an interview partnership? How did others respond to our work? Would we want to work together again? They must also evaluate the process itself: How did the final decision-making team work? Did we fall into groupthink? Was our hiring decision accepted by the entire group?

Team interviews help us hire smart and keep 'em. If we create strong team partnerships, we can strengthen our interview process. The next chapter will explore the legal issues that face all interviewers whether interviewing solo, in teams, or on panels

PRACTICE EXERCISE

Read the following statement by a team member and identify which stage of team development each team is in: (a) forming, (b) storming, (c) norming, (d) performing, or (e) adjourning.

1. "Who is in charge in this group?"
2. "I couldn't possiblly add anything to the good overview Mark provided to the group."
3. "If we had it to do over, what would we do differently?"
4. "Now that we know that Mary is really good at discovery and James can do the summary, I'd like to volunteer to do the due diligence."
5. "To get us started, let's talk a few minutes informally."
6. "I know more about this process than my partner because I've had to do it so many times in the past."
7. "Don't let Janice talk too much about her alma mater or we'll be here all day. When it comes to that topic, she's unstoppable."
8. "I was so impressed by that candidate, and I can tell that each of you agree with me. She really wowed us, didn't she?"

See Appendix A for answers.

FIVE

Keeping the Interview Legal

In the previous chapters we defined strategic interviewing, and we talked about the importance of digging deeper to get at the truth. We looked at behavior-based interviewing as a technique to accomplish this goal and at the power of team interviewing. One of the important considerations for today's manager or interviewer is how she can get at the truth and still keep the interview legal. Over the years an increasing number of touchy situations have arisen in the interview environment that border on crossing the legal line. In this chapter we will examine the effects of legal issues on a strategic interview, the legal realities, high-risk areas, and what you can do as an interviewer to avoid legal landmines.

One of the principle reasons companies hesitate to allow managers to interview is they fear the manager will violate legal standards. Human resource professionals are trained to conduct legal interviews, but they may not be trained to hire smart. If you want to hire smart, it is important for others in the organization, beyond human resources, to learn how to interview legally. The recipe for doing so is not so complicated that others cannot learn how.

I discussed these issues in my previous book, *Strategic Interviewing: Skills and Tactics for Savvy Executives*.[1] Not much has changed since that book was published in 2000. Nonetheless, today's world includes not simply face-to-face interviews but also electronic communication. In this chapter we'll expand our analysis of the legal issues by exploring the sensitive areas that arise with email communication and with webcam interviewing. Neither of these areas has been tested legally, but a good commonsense approach will prevent you from getting tangled up in murky legal waters.

THE REALITIES

In years past, fewer sensitive legal areas existed (certainly none related to email and Skype), but in the 1960s that list grew exponentially. One reason for this growth was a new diversity of family life that created an accompanying diversity in the workplace. Today those diversity changes are so embedded in our culture that the new generation of Millennials take them for granted. Nonetheless, some managers persist in asking questions that border on discriminatory. Candidates come to interviews highly informed. They've learned what's appropriate and what's not from their college placement offices or from online sites. When we violate the legal standards, we not only threaten the company with potential lawsuits but we also show a lack of professionalism.

Diversity of Family Life

Today more single parents are rearing children alone. According to *Custodial Mothers and Fathers and Their Child Support: 2007*, released by the U.S. Census Bureau in November 2009,[2] approximately 13.7 million single parents have custody of 21.8 million children under 21 years of age. More than one-quarter (26.3%) of all children under 21 years of age live with one of their parents while the other parent lives outside the home. These statistics probably startle you, but if you look around at your own family, you probably can attest to their truth. In years past, not only did the wife stay home and take care of the kids and perform other household duties, but also grandparents, aunts, and uncles lived nearby. Today more and more people live miles from their extended families. Single parents face rearing their children without the support of other family members. Furthermore, as parents become aged, they migrate to their children's nest for care. Many families not only face dealing with their children but also providing care to aged parents. This means that people are staying in the workforce longer in order to financially support their children and to help support their aging parents.

Diversity of the Workplace

With more single parents working, the workplace had to change. Today's workplace is more responsive to the needs of working mothers and fathers by providing child care options, insurance options that allow for daycare, family planning options, lenient maternity and paternity leaves, flexible hours, and work-at-home options. The list goes on. The increase in the number of women in the workplace further complicates these changes. Statistics show that in 1950 about one in three women participated in the labor force.[3] According to the *Economist*, women now make up over half of American workers (59.2%).

Figure 5.1   Women's Labor Force Participation Rates, Selected Countries, 1970–2009 (See http://www.census.gov/prod/2009pubs/p60-237.pdf).

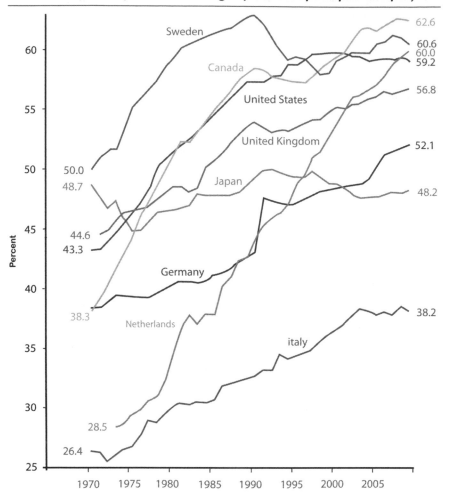

Furthermore, "[women] run some of the world's best companies, such as PepsiCo, Archer Daniels Midland and W.L. Gore. They earn nearly sixty percent of university degrees in America and Europe."[4] In other words, the workplace is no longer a male-dominated environment but instead consists of both men and women. "Take a look at Figure 5.1 which shows the rise in Women's Labor Force Participation Rates by country."

Sexual diversity is only one part of the diversity issue. Another major change in the workplace is cultural diversity. We've become a global village. That means we not only have more people from other nationalities and cultures in our workplace, but we, too, are working in places far away from our 50 states.

Most major companies have holdings in China, Southeast Asia, or India as well as Europe and South America. The U.S. labor statistics tell us that foreign-born workers make up almost half of the net increase in the U.S. labor force.[5]

With all these changes come increases in the number of lawsuits. According to a blog titled *Diversity in the Workplace*, in the last 10 years a growing number of employees filed lawsuits charging that employers discriminated against them on the basis of race, gender, age, or physical disability. The caseload at the federal Equal Employment Opportunity Commission more than tripled from 1991 to 1998 and continues to rise. These lawsuits clog the courts. What this means to today's interviewer is that there has been a s ignificant rise in the number of legal protections against hiring, promotion, demotion, and firing abuses.[6] The lawsuits, therefore, create more legal restrictions in the interview environment.

MISBEHAVIOR OF THE PAST

As you look at the changes in family life and in the workplace, you may wonder ask why you can't ask certain questions. For example, why can't you ask candidates about child care or whether they intend to marry? Clearly, with more single parents in the workplace, these would seem legitimate probe areas. In fact, *questions related to a person's marital status or how that person plans to take care of children during the workday are considered violations of the person's privacy.*

Many questions interviewers may have routinely asked in years past now fall into sensitive areas and must be avoided. Interviewers used to ask certain people of different races or sexes questions that they didn't ask others. Those questions felt intrusive and insulting to the candidates, and they objected. Because of these abuses, lawsuits emerged and the courts took action. In today's interview environment, you must avoid sensitive areas and show respect for the candidate's right to privacy.

According to the United States Employment Opportunity Commission, the following laws currently shape what we can and cannot ask in an interview:

- Equal Pay Act of 1963
- Title VII, Civil Rights Act, 1964
- Immigration Reform and Control Act, 1986
- Age Discrimination in Employment Act
- Vocational Rehabilitation Act
- Vietnam Era Veteran's Readjustment Assistant Act
- Privacy Act, 1974
- Fair Credit and Reporting Act, 1970

- Family Education Rights and Privacy Act and Buckley Amendment, 1974
- Freedom of Information Act, 1966
- American Disabilities Act

The Civil Rights Act protects people from discrimination against race and national origin; the Age Discrimination Act protects people against discrimination because of age; the American Disabilities Act protects people from discrimination based on handicaps. The Fair Credit and Reporting Act prevents you from asking people about their credit rating. The Privacy Act protects people from giving you information about their private life, including family planning. The list is long and is getting longer.

WHAT QUESTIONS TO ASK AND WHAT QUESTIONS NOT TO ASK

Whenever an interviewer faces a candidate, whether she conducts a structured, laissez-faire, or strategic interview, the possibility for legal issues exist. With a strategic interview, your goal is to dig deeply in order to uncover the truth. If while you are digging you step on a legal landmine, you must change directions. In other works, you must give up that line of questioning and go somewhere else. For interview purposes, however, *there is nothing illegal in listening*. If a candidate voluntarily tells you something that you did not ask for, you did nothing wrong. But there are two things you do not want to do if this should happen to you:

1. Panic and say something to the candidate that closes that person down.
2. Probe deeper.

For example,

Interviewer: Tell me what interests you about moving to this area of the South?

Candidate: My family is from South America. When we first came here, we settled in Texas. My aunts live here and some cousins. I have lived far from them over the last two years. I'm ready to come back. We have a strong family culture, being from Argentina. I've missed that.

Interviewer: I see on your résumé that you supervised five people in your last job. What did you find rewarding with supervision?

The interviewer began with a very safe question, but the candidate answered by talking about his nationality and his culture. He gave the interviewer a lot of information in that response that the interviewer might have ordinarily followed up on, but instead the interviewer led the interview down a very different path: supervision. Had the interviewer persisted with a probe, "What do you enjoy about being with your family?" or with a paraphrase, "So family life is very important to you," the candidate may have elaborated further, and you don't want that. If the interviewer had panicked and said, "You really shouldn't be telling me anything about your family. Let's move on to another area," the candidate might have held back, thinking he did something wrong

Even though the interviewer in this example did not asked a specifically illegal question, she entered dangerous territory. As a professional interviewer, you do not want to give the perception of asking illegal questions. You wouldn't want this candidate to leave this interview and say, "All she did was ask me about my family and my country."

The interview guide in Table 5.1 will help you determine what questions you can and cannot ask. The high-risk areas noted are typical of laws throughout the United States. In other words, most states follow these guidelines, but if you have any questions, consult your corporate attorney or another lawyer who specializes in labor laws because there are variations from state to state.

Perhaps you see a trend in this list: there are some things that you can never ask, race, national origin, sex, but there are other things that you can ask if they are job related. Olsen explained this phenomenon by using the legal term, BOQ, which means *bona fide qualification for the occupation.*[7] Olsen told us there are two kinds of qualifications for any job: that which is required and that which is preferred. We talked about these qualification types in Chapter 2 when we discussed writing job descriptions. Olsen explained that if something is required for the job but under usual circumstances would be problematic legally, you can ask it. If it is simply useful or preferred in the job, do not ask it. This then is the simple litmus test: *job relatedness.* Does the person *have to have* this skill, ability, or knowledge to do the job?

A perfect example of BOQ affects the issue of pregnancy. In more than 99 percent of the interviews you might conduct, you would never ask a woman if she was pregnant or planning to get pregnant. If, however, you work in an environment where dangerous chemicals might affect the safety of a fetus, then you can ask this question or at least inform the candidate that such conditions exist. Although this is an extreme case, it illustrates the importance of job relatedness. All jobs are different, and that makes it difficult to say *never.* You must consider your jobs and ask yourself if this trait, skill, or information is essential to performance.

If you are worried about whether or not a person will report to work every day on time, probe issues that explore what kind of transportation he has and what options he has available when his primary form of transportation is nonfunctional. Do not ask about his religion or the number of children he is responsible for.

In strategic interviews where the interviewer is digging beyond the superficial information, you can expect to uncover sensitive information. Your job

Table 5.1   Legally What Questions to Ask and What Questions Not to Ask

High-Risk Area	Lawful Questions	Unlawful Questions
Name	"What other names might you have used?"	"That's an unusual name. Where are you from?" Any questions related to lineage, ancestry or national origin.
Marital and Family	"What obstacles do you have for working weekends?"	"How many children do you have in elementary school?" Any questions related to marital status or number of children.
Pregnancy	"We deal with some hazardous materials. What are your plans for starting a family?"	"Are you pregnant?" Never ask about a candidate's family plans unless the workplace could prove dangerous to a fetus.
Age	"You must be eighteen to work here. How old are you? Minors must show proof of age.	"What year did you graduate from high school?" If asked of an older candidate, this is illegal. Never discuss age or ask for proof of age from older candidates.
Handicaps	"The job requires lifting fifty pounds or more. What difficulties might you have performing that task?"	"What physical or mental handicaps do you have?" Any general questions about health or physical disabilities.
Sex	Never ask.	"You mention a partner. What is your sexual preference?" Never ask about sex or sexual preference, and do not assume a certain sex can or cannot perform certain jobs (e.g., heavy lifting).
Race	Never ask.	"Are you an American Indian or from India?" Never ask a question about a person's race.
Military Record	"What courses did you take while in the Army?"	"Were you discharged honorably?"
Photo	"Please send us a photo for our employee newsletter."	"Please send us a photo with your application." Never ask for a photo before hiring.
Citizenship	"Are you allowed to work in the United States? If so, please	"Are your parents U.S. citizens?" Never probe the country of citizenship, the nature of citizenship,

(*continued*)

Table 5.1 (continued)

High-Risk Area	Lawful Questions	Unlawful Questions
	present proof of citizenship."	or the person's lineage. A simple "Where are you from?" could be a dangerous question.
Nationality	"What languages do you speak?" (if speaking a foreign language is part of the job).	"I see you're not a native of the United States. Where are you from?" Never ask about nationality or a candidate's "mother tongue."
Education	"Tell me about your experiences in school." Any question about classes or school activities.	"I see you went to a Catholic college. What made you choose that school?" Never ask questions about a national-, racial-, or religious-affiliation school.
Experience	All work experience questions are legally acceptable.	
Conviction, Arrest, and Court Record	"Have you had any felony convictions?"	"How many times have you had to appear in court or been arrested?" Never ask about arrests or court appearances.
Relatives	"What relatives do you have working for our company?"	"Where do your parents live and work?"
Organizations	"What offices did you hold in your professional organization?"	"Are you a member of any unions?" Never request a list of clubs or societies a person belongs to. Never ask about union affiliation.
Religion	"What might prevent you from working on Sundays?"	"Are you a member of a faith that would prevent you from working any day of the week?" Never ask about a religious affiliation.
Credit Rating	"Because this job requires you to collect money, how is your credit?"	Never ask about credit rating, garnishments, or charge accounts unless the job requires the person to handle money or trust funds.

For a complete list of what to ask and what not to ask, see http://www.doi. gov/hrm/pmanager/st13c4.html.

as an interviewer is to recognize those sensitive areas and direct the interview down another path.

Let's examine an example of a strategic interview that went wrong:

Interviewer: My name is Nancy Morris. Thank you for coming today. I'm an information analyst for the company and want to ask you several questions. From your résumé I see you are still in school.

Candidate: Yes, I am scheduled to finish in April. I thought I'd better start looking for a job soon because I'm a single mom and I want to have something lined up as soon as my teaching assistantship is over.

Interviewer: I'm a single mom, too. It's not easy taking care of the kids and going to work every day. How did you handle all your responsibilities when you were in school?

Candidate: Actually, I had some help. We have a very strong church. There's a program there that is designed to help single parents with their kids. Some of the people who participate are nurses or work strange shifts, and others, like me, are out during the day. We take turns staffing the children's care center. It's great because I know the church people and trust them and it costs me almost nothing.

Interviewer: Gosh, that sounds wonderful. I wish I went to a church like that—

Candidate: You can. It's the First Baptist Church of Main Street. We'd love to see you.

Interviewer: Thanks. I'll check it out. Now tell me about what made you decide to major in finance?

Candidate: I worked as a bookkeeper for a big organization as a volunteer when I was in high school. My parents thought it would be good experience for me. As it turned out, I really enjoyed the job. When I went to school, it was natural for me to look for a career related to bookkeeping, but when I didn't enjoy accounting, finance became a natural choice.

Interviewer: What organization was that where you began working as a bookkeeper?

Candidate: I didn't put it on my résumé because it was a volunteer job, and it was while I was in high school. The organization was connected to my dad's union at the Ford plant. I not only learned about bookkeeping, but I also saw the value of people working together for a common cause. It was very inspiring for me as a young person and gave me impetus to do some of the volunteer things I do now.

Interviewer: What kinds of volunteer things do you do now?

Candidate: I work hard for the National Human Rights organization, particularly focused on the needs of women, and for the Cancer Society. I haven't been as active this year because I was finishing up my school work, but I plan to help with their fundraising drives this summer.

Interviewer: You were president of the National Finance Organization for students while in school. Tell me about some of that work.

Candidate: I was elected last year and have enjoyed the opportunity to work with many of the students across campus. It's been quite a challenge.

Interviewer: I was president of our national organization when I was in school and sometimes found students not too reliable. What difficulties did you have getting people to do the work?

Candidate: For the most part people were cooperative. We had a big event last Christmas to organize around donating gifts for underprivileged kids. I learned about the program through my church and floated it to the group. Most people were supportive and helpful. There was one guy who said he opposed any kind of welfare, and he refused to participate.

Interviewer: That must have been frustrating for you.

Candidate: It was at first because he was such a loud dissenter. But we managed to get enough people involved that we collected over 50 gifts for the kids. I was very proud about that. In fact, I met my fiancé through this effort. He also was majoring in finance, but he's a year younger than I am.

Interviewer: How was it working with a group of people like that?

Candidate: I like working in groups. Having a lot of support makes a big difference. Matt, my fiancé, took up the slack when I had other priorities, like dealing with the kids or something. The nice thing about working with others is people help each other out.

Interviewer: What other things did you find rewarding working in a group?

Candidate: Just the stimulation of sharing ideas. We used to brainstorm together a lot. That was fun. I suppose I'm more of a team player than one who likes to work alone. Of course, in finance I have to spend time alone with the figures, but today's economy tends to encourage people to get creative. That's where it's fun working in teams.

Interviewer: It sounds as if you've had a lot of experience working in teams.

Candidate: Many of our classes required us to work together on projects.

Interviewer: Tell me about some of the frustrations you had with teamwork. I know it's fun and stimulating, but it can also be hard.

Analysis of Interview

Nancy Morris conducted a strategic interview using the POINT process, but was the interview legal?

First, her initial introduction was short and clear. She began by asking the candidate about her school work. When the candidate mentioned she was a single mom, Nancy's antenna should have shot up. Instead she responded with, "I'm a single mom, too. It's not easy taking care of the kids and going to work every day. How did you handle all your responsibilities when you were in school?" Here are the good points about this follow-up:

- She shared a bit of information about herself to create rapport with the candidate early in the interview. This is a strategy we use in the POINT process.
- She asked a question that clearly aligned with a target competency—how the candidate manages multiple tasks.
- She asked an open question that "piggy-backed" on what the candidate said.

Notwithstanding these good points, *Nancy made a fatal mistake—she followed up in a legally sensitive area.* The question, "How did you manage all your responsibilities when you were in school?" could be construed as illegal. Nancy appears to be asking how the candidate managed to care for her children and go to school. This is clearly illegal and could be contested.

Note that even a well-designed strategic response can prove illegal if you chose to follow up in a high-risk area.

Going further into the interview, Nancy listened a lot and allowed the candidate to talk. The candidate told her about her church and the child care program there. Once that line of questioning started, Nancy should have gotten out of it as soon as possible. Instead she stepped deeper into a touchy area by, saying, "I wish I went to a church like that." Finally, when Nancy said, "Now tell me what made you decide to major in finance," she extricated herself from a very dangerous situation. But was it too late?

Remember, being legal in an interview is not simply about the questions you ask; it's also about the perception of legality. This candidate will likely walk away from this interview and say to someone else, "The interviewer seemed very interested in how I managed to go to school and take care of my kids."

Later the candidate began talking about her volunteer work. This information seemed safe enough until Nancy made another fatal mistake by asking about the organization where the candidate volunteered. This question put Nancy in another critical area: she probed the candidate about that organization and other organizations she worked with. She didn't actually ask about the organizations, but again a lot of time was spent talking about outside organizations. Not until Nancy steered the interview away by asking about the candidate's particular professional organization was she again on safe ground.

Once Nancy began probing the candidate's work with groups, she kept things safe. When the candidate mentioned a fiancé, Nancy did not probe that relationship. Instead she kept the interview focused on team work and the pros and cons of working with people. Notice in the last part of the interview the careful way Nancy avoided high-risk areas. She needed to do that throughout the interview.

In the final analysis this interview was clearly highly strategic, but it was also highly illegal. Nancy needed to refocus the interview immediately when the candidate mentioned being a single mom and later when the candidate mentioned working with outside organizations.

Part of the job of any strategic interviewer requires you to listen for your target competencies as well as legally sensitive areas. If a sensitive area arises around one of your target competencies, you must get at that competency in another way. Therein lies the challenge Nancy did not meet.

What Are the Chances This Candidate Will Sue Nancy?

One concern that faces all managers and the companies they work for is the likelihood of a lawsuit. Indeed, as we noted earlier, many of the restrictions you face in interviews arose out of improper interviews in years past and the creation of laws to protect us from those kinds of questions. Given these concerns and our past misbehavior in the interview environment, you must stay alert to the legal ramifications when you explore high-risk areas with candidates. Nonetheless the likelihood that the candidate will sue Nancy is weak.

Candidates come to employers with one goal in mind. They want a job. They do not come with the intent to trick an interviewer into saying something illegal and then to file a lawsuit. Because candidates want a job, they are likely to ignore illegal questions. They know if they file a lawsuit against the company, they will never work for that company or probably in that industry. What makes it even more unlikely candidates will sue you is that these cases are usually your word against theirs. Nancy can always deny that she asked anything illegal (and she did just ask one question that was clearly illegal). If Nancy had interviewed with a partner, she and the partner could deny any wrongdoing. Candidates do not have the financial resources to sue companies for improper interviewing. Companies often employ corporate lawyers who protect them and their employees. Individuals do not have such safeguards.

And yet you want to avoid any chance for a lawsuit. Do you want to serve as a test case for your company? Do you want to face having to justify your line of questioning to your corporate attorney? Furthermore, you cannot overlook the fact that if you violate the law enough times, it will catch up with you. When people join together in litigation—a class-action suit—your chances of success in the courtroom diminish. Finally, by asking clearly illegal questions or allowing the interview to digress down illegal paths, interviewers appear unprofessional. Candidates know what is legally sound and what isn't. You do not want to get a reputation for treading in legally sensitive areas.

Although the chances of a lawsuit are slim, it could happen if you ignore the high-risk areas. If, however, you pay attention to what you can and cannot ask and keep an eye on the new laws that emerge, you will be fine. Job relatedness is the key to success. Always ask yourself, "Is this something I have to know to determine if the person can do the job?"

THE DO'S AND DON'TS OF SKYPE AND EMAIL INTERVIEWING

The onset of technology brings new challenges for maintaining a professional, legal interview. Issues related to the new methods for screening candidates have not been legally tested, but you want to exercise common sense and avoid anything that others might consider discriminatory. Here are some tips.

- Keep your emails professional. It is easy in an email to relax your guard because email communication feels less formal than a written letter. Questions about family and mutual acquaintances might prove dangerous. Treat your email correspondence as you would a written letter. Remember emails are traceable and admissible in court.
- Be careful when you use the "Reply All" button in an email. Always remember who the people are in that chain and consider whether the reply is something you wish everyone to see.
- Never send a rejection by email. If a candidate sends an unsolicited résumé, you may respond by email either directing that candidate to the appropriate ways to submit an application or letting him know you are not recruiting. *But any candidate who has made it through the first part of the screening process must receive written notification of rejection, not an email.*
- Unless you initiate a new email each time you correspond with a candidate, the candidate can see the trail of correspondence. If you want to keep that trail visible, that's fine. But if you prefer to respond without the trail, you must start a new email each time. This is a good method for keeping your responses professional. Often when you have a trail, you tend to send shorter responses that might prove more informal and more legally dangerous.

SIX

How to Create Trust in the Interview

As we move deeper into the POINT process, we turn our attention to trust. Having seen how important it is to keep the interview legal, you must not let legal restrictions keep you from delving into a strategic interview. As noted, you must stay alert to the high-risk areas and change directions whenever those areas surface. One of the most difficult things for an interviewer to do is create trust without violating privacy.

Olson talked about the importance of openness in the interview when he created an interview process he called PROBE. The O in Olson's scheme stood for keeping the interview open by using open questions. He did not go the next step, namely to create a system for interviewers to understand the psychological benefits for creating trust.

This chapter explores the *O in the POINT process: openness*. We'll look at how to open the interview and keep it open. Once you create openness, you are more likely to establish trust. When candidates are closed or tight-lipped, they tend to hold back information. Your goal as a strategic interviewer is to facilitate opportunities to share.

We will begin to explore openness by examining the purpose of trust in the interview. Why is trust important? To answer that question we'll explore the work of two psychologists, Joseph Luft and Harrington Ingham. Luft and Ingham developed a model for social interaction based on human behavior. They published this model in the late 1960s and called it the Johari window.[1] I have made reference to the Johari window in nearly every management and leadership workshop I've taught as well as referred to it in two of my books (*Strategic Interviewing: Skills and Tactics for Savvy Executives* and *The New Handshake: Sales Meets Social Media*). Why do I like this model so much? Luft and Ingham took a very complex subject, namely human interaction, and explained it in a clear, practical way.

- Do not enter into an online chat with a candidate. Chat sessions tend to be informal and may put you in a position where you find yourself talking about family, friends, or mutual organizations, which are high-risk areas.

- Never ask for a photo. If you wish to find a candidate on the social media sites such as Facebook or LinkedIn where photos exist, search for them under their names. Do not ask them for the links to those sites.

- When interviewing with Skype or other webcam technology, make sure the candidate knows who is in the room. Make all appropriate introductions.

- Do not tape an interview without the candidate's permission. Most webcam technology provide easy recording mechanisms. Just as with secretly taping an interview, it could be illegal to secretly record a video interview.

- If you prescreen with Skype or other video technology with one candidate, you must do so with all candidates. Otherwise Skype might appear to be a subtle way of asking for a photo. For example, if two of your candidates are local and you screen by telephone without photos, and two live far away and you screen by video, it could appear that the two local candidates had an unfair advantage. Instead, conduct the two local interviews either face-to-face or with Skype. *It's ideal to use the same medium with all candidates*. Doing so will avoid any question about why you chose one medium for one and not another.

- Skype may not feel like a "real" interview, but it is. All the high-risk areas that we discussed in this chapter apply to Skype interviewing.

- If a candidate is interviewing at home on Skype and a child or spouse enters the room, do not ask about that person. In other words, do not say, "Is that your daughter? She's adorable." If the candidate tells you "This is my daughter" or "This is my wife," that's fine. But try to steer the interview back to pertinent questions; do not engage in a conversation with the family members.

PRACTICE EXERCISE

Read the following interview and answer the questions at the end.

Interviewer: Thank you for joining me on Skype this morning. I hope you are comfortable with this medium.

Candidate: Actually, I'm an old coot when it comes to technology. I just missed the generation that feels at ease, but my son helped me set this up. Can you see me okay?

Interviewer: I can see you fine. Just let me know if you have any issues as we go along. I know what you mean by the technology. It's hard until you get used to it. I, too, had a steep learning curve.

Candidate: You got that right. Even email is a mystery to me. I've got friends who only email, but not me. And I'm never going to mess with Facebook. I'm past that world.

Interviewer: When you say "past that world," what do you mean?

Candidate: I mean at 52 I don't intend to waste my time on something like Facebook. I've got more important things to do.

Interviewer: So you think younger people have more time for learning the new technology? Why is that?

Candidate: They have more time for everything. Life gets more precious as you get older. That's one reason I want to change jobs. I'm looking for something where I can look forward to going to work.

Interviewer: What kind of job would that be?

Candidate: For one thing, less travel. I've lived on the road long enough. I want to spend more time with my family. I have a grandchild now. That really affected me. Being gone three to four days a week is not my definition of a good job.

Interviewer: I don't have grandchildren yet, but I do have a young daughter. I know what you mean. It's very hard to leave her when I go to work every morning.

Candidate: (Laughs) My wife keeps volunteering to babysit for my granddaughter so I know what you mean. It takes all my discipline to walk out that door and leave them. Sometimes I wish I didn't have to. My wife wants me to stop travelling, too. She keeps nagging me about it.

Interviewer: How much travel would you find acceptable?

Candidate: For one thing, never on the weekends. My current job requires me to leave on Sundays. I never get to go to church with the family. That is something I want to change.

Interviewer: So attending church on Sundays is important to you.

Candidate: That and being there for my family. When I was younger, work was the top priority. Now things have changed. Family is number one. That doesn't make work unimportant; it just changes the priority. Does that make sense?

Interviewer: Of course. Family comes first. I get it.

Did this interviewer keep the interview legal? Check those that apply.

1. Interviewer asked questions related to the candidate's age.
2. Interviewer asked questions related to the candidate's marital status or future marital plans.
3. Interviewer asked questions related to children, child ⟨ ments, or how the spouse feels about the candidate work weekends.
4. Interviewer asked questions related to the candidate's arres
5. Interviewer asked questions about the candidate's birthplace ship.
6. Interviewer asked questions about the candidate's race, natio. religion, church attended, or religious holidays.
7. Interviewer asked questions related to the candidate's credit h
8. Interviewer asked the candidate if she was pregnant.
9. Interviewer asked the candidate how he feels about labor un previous status with labor unions.

See Appendix A for answers and an analysis of this interview.

The second aim of this chapter is to enable you, the interviewer, to break down barriers that prevent openness. You'll see how important it is to interview the entire person, not simply the person at work. And finally you will learn how to effectively employ icebreakers in the interview.

Openness is the strategic interviewer's way to let go of the interview reigns. The goal is to loosen up the interview to allow for more candid discussion on both sides of the table. Recalling how a laissez-faire interview can get out of hand, the strategic interviewer applies the skills of openness without turning the interview into a laissez-faire experience. In other words, as you relax and open up yourself to create trust, you must also maintain control, just as when guiding a horse home you let loose your tight hold on the reigns, but you keep them within reach. Maintaining this balance is all part of the challenge of keeping the interview open.

By the end of this chapter you will have a clear understanding of why openness is important, what kinds of challenges the interview environment presents in terms of creating openness, as well as how to go about breaking down the barriers by using such tools as icebreakers.

THE JOHARI WINDOW

Figure 6.1 presents four quadrants. Luft and Ingham told us that all people interact with one another based on these four quadrants. In other words the quadrants open and close according to the relationships you have with the individuals with whom you interact.

Quadrant 1: Open Area

The first quadrant represents that part of you that is known to others and known to yourself. As an interviewer, you want to increase the size of this quadrant. If the open area represents a tiny portion of the person's Johari window, you will learn little about that person. Indeed, you will have a more difficult time trying to delve beyond the superficial. Imagine a scenario where you walk into a networking meeting in which you face hundreds of people you've never met. When you interact with those people, shake their hands, and begin talking, how large is your open area? How large might you predict their open areas to be? It is likely you will learn surface information about each individual but not much more. In the interview environment, however, you want to go beyond that surface area. You may not get too deep, but you want to chip away at the surface. Clearly, just like in a networking event, you would not expect the open area to be wide open. You wouldn't expect, for example, a candidate to waltz into your office and begin telling you about his divorce or the time he got caught cheating in school. But in time, you would expect him to relax enough to tell you how things really felt at his last job or if his previous boss micromanaged him.

Figure 6.1   The four quadrants of the Johari Window

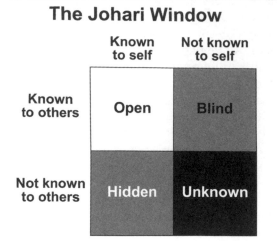

The Johari Window

Quadrant 2: Blind Area

This is the part of the Johari window where others know things about you that you do not know about yourself. These kinds of blind spots surface in an interview all the time. They are things you do not see yourself, but others see and sometimes even reveal to you. Until you hear the message, however, the behaviors remain in your blind area. When a candidate uses the words *like* or *you know* excessively or fiddles with her pen, she's unaware of these behaviors because they are blind spots. Strategic interviewers make note of these blind spots and recognize that they could present a problem if the person were hired. The jumpy eyes you notice in the interview may not disturb the interview, but they may disturb a colleague or a client in the work environment. The blind area includes not only these kinds of behavioral tics but also communication behaviors, such as the candidate who clearly doesn't listen to your questions or the candidate who interrupts you. Again, these behaviors may not adversely affect the interview, but they could present enormous problems once the candidate becomes an employee.

Strategic interviewers often do not point out the blind spots to candidates. Imagine for a moment you are the person who constantly interrupts. Who are the people who could reveal that behavior in a way that you would hear it? Luft and Ingham found that not just anyone can point out another person's blind spots. The people in the best position to do so are the people a person *respects*. If the person does not respect you or if she do not respect you enough, she will not hear what you tell her, and she will continue to interrupt. It takes time to build true respect. Often interviewers are not with candidates long enough to create that kind of respect. If you point out a blind spot to a candidate before you build sufficient respect, you threaten to tear down all the trust you might have created, and the candidate will likely move back behind her walls.

Interviewers, on the other hand, can show openness to candidates by hearing when they point out one of the interviewers' own blind spots. If a candidate gives you a nonverbal cue (usually candidates won't tell you a blind spot outright) suggesting you did something offensive, do you see it? If you catch that cue and respond, you'll come a long way in developing trust because you will have shown the candidate respect.

Quadrant 3: Hidden Area

The third section of the Johari window is the most important section to an interview environment. Quadrant 3 represents those things the candidate knows about himself but you do not know; that is, the things known to self but not known to others. It's all the stuff you as a strategic interviewer want to uncover. The hidden area, as Luft and Ingham called it, includes everything the candidate doesn't want you to unearth. It might be as simple as the town he grew up in or as complex as the fact that he was fired from his last job.

Again, think about your own hidden area. Who are the people with whom you share your secrets? Aren't they the people you trust? The interviewer expects a candidate to share hidden information even though trust hasn't been established. As an interviewer you ask deep questions of people you hardly know and expect them to fully open up to you. That's the nature of the interview.

From the initial handshake, the interviewer must establish trust. Candidates come into the interview wary. The interviewer and the candidate harbor hidden agendas in their hidden areas. Barriers exist on both sides of the table.

Therefore, while *respect* is a keyword to reveal blind spots, *trust* is the keyword to reveal information in the hidden area. Without trust, the strategic interviewer can give up trying to dig deeper than the superficial, and the candidate will remain firmly behind closed doors.

Quadrant 4: Unknown Area

This area represents what is not known to oneself nor to others—the unknown area. As psychologists Luft and Harriman recognized, there are things that no one knows—things that reside in our subconscious. Those unknown things stay hidden deep in the subconscious unless there is a strong amount of *respect and trust* in the human relationship to uncover them.

The employment interview environment is not a place where "aha" moments often happen. They could happen, but they are not something the interviewer expects. *The goal of the interview is to break down the barriers enough to learn more than superficial information, not to uncover what might exist in someone's subconscious.* Therefore it is unlikely that you will release information from the unknown area. Just know it exists.

HOW THE JOHARI WINDOW WORKS IN AN INTERVIEW

Let's read the following scenario and stop at times to imagine what the Johari window looks like at that point in the interview.

Louise Jones walks into the interview room where she is interviewing for a management-level position with a large computer software firm. She meets Mark Basin, her interviewer.

Mark rises and shakes Louise's hand, saying, "Thank you for coming downtown to our offices. I know how hard it is to negotiate traffic in a new town. I hope you didn't find it too daunting. My name is Mark Basin, but please call me Mark. May I call you Louise?"

"Oh, yes, please do."

How might you describe the Johari window for Louise at this moment? It's likely that Louise has a very small open area and a large hidden area. She's probably thinking things like, "I hope I can impress this interviewer," or "I sure could use this job. It would be a great boost in my career," or "I wonder how long this interview will take." These kinds of thoughts suggest typical apprehension at the outset of any interview. If Mark understands the concepts behind the Johari window, he will know what to do to help break through some of Louise's barriers.

"Please take a seat," Mark says, motioning to the chair across from his desk. "We're going to talk informally for a few minutes, and then I want you to meet my colleague, Jamie DiAngelo, who works in the sales department. I work primarily in the area of acquisitions, where I see you've had a lot of experience."

"I have, actually," Louise says. "My current job focuses on acquisitions for our global sites."

"Your current company is French, right?"

"The parent company is from Lyons. That makes working for them very interesting."

"I worked for a French company when I was fresh out of college. They sent me to Paris for a 10-day visit. I was totally blown away. Have you had opportunities to go to France?"

"As a matter of fact, I just returned from a trip two weeks ago. I've been several times since I've been working for Bijoux. You're right. It's like being in another world. I love it."

Have you noticed a crack in Louise's open area? Mark is working to loosen her up. The conversation about France accomplished two things: first, it enabled Mark to share a little something about himself, and second, it was something easy to talk about. Mark decided not to dig too deeply yet. If he had tried to dig deeper this early in the interview, Louise would have closed up.

When Louise shifts back in her seat, Mark says, "Describe some of the differences you noticed in France from the United States."

"For one thing, they seem to function like a small town everywhere, even in Paris. The French go to the market every morning for fresh food. Their refrigerators are tiny. It took me a while to realize that they don't stock up on food. Instead they eat what's fresh every day. Also, the lifestyle seems slower, particularly in Lyons. I enjoyed the fact that people didn't seem to be on a strict time crunch. They are aware of being where they need to be, but they seem less concerned about hours. At first it drove me nuts, but then I got into the groove. Lunch, for example, can last a couple of hours, but then they'll work till seven or eight at night."

"So how was it for you, Louise, not having a strict eight-to-five schedule?"

"Like I say at first I was a bit stressed by it because I didn't know what was expected of me. But after a while I stopped worrying about it and just enjoyed doing whatever I was doing. I became much more focused on the task at hand instead of constantly looking at my watch."

"Sounds like that might have been an 'aha' moment for you."

She smiles. "In a way. I tried to bring some of those ideas back here, but the culture here is so different. It doesn't seem to work as well."

"Tell me how you tried to bring the ideas back."

Mark is on a roll now. He's asking good strategic questions and clearly focusing on some of his target competencies. Louise is doing a lot of talking. By focusing on her experience in France, Mark enabled her to open up about something she seemed to enjoy. At this early stage in the interview, he is still careful not to push too hard or touch on areas that might cause defensiveness. We can see Louise's open area opening more as we learn about her and the way she likes to work. But so far we have not learned anything of significance from her hidden area.

Louise answers, "One thing I tried to do is quit being so focused myself on time issues. My job with Bijoux requires that I supervise three other people. I'm responsible for their work product. After having been in France, it was clear to me that people can be productive even when they are on different work schedules. One of my employees was constantly late. He strolled in 30 minutes late every morning. I talked to him and tried to help him see the importance of adhering to a strict work schedule. He'd do okay for a week or so, but then he'd slip back again. It was driving me nuts."

"What was it that troubled you so much?"

Louise takes a deep breath. "One day I asked myself that same question. I had to admit he did a good job. In fact, as far as productivity went, he was my best employee and the most likely to get promoted—that is, if I recommended him. But I didn't feel I could recommend him if he didn't come in on time. That bothered me a lot. After I came back from France, I realized that the problem was more mine than his. I wasn't so much upset that he came in late as I was with the feeling that he didn't respect me as a supervisor. He seemed to be testing the limits with me, and that annoyed me."

Mark got into some deep issues here. Louise probably did not intend to tell Mark all about her frustration with this employee, but that information was flowing out of her. The more she talked, the more she revealed about herself as a supervisor. What has happened is Mark is releasing information from Louise's hidden area as her open area widens. Notice how little Mark has talked. We can guess that he gave Louise good eye contact and lots of nonverbal cues that encouraged her to continue talking (head nods, "Oh, yes, I see's").

Mark continues: "Being tested like that would have bothered me, too. How did you deal with wanting to promote him but sensing he didn't respect you?"

"I just let go. I did what we did in France. I stopped talking to him about coming in late and focused on our projects. I noticed that he often stayed later or worked over the weekends to finish something by a deadline. And, miracle of all miracles, he started coming in on time without me saying anything."

"Wow! I bet that made you proud."

"Yeah, in a way. It taught me that we can learn from our European friends. Of course I'm still time conscious, but no more with this employee. He was eventually promoted with my recommendation."

Mark did a great job with letting Louise tell him about this situation. He listened with intent, trying to keep her talking but also pursuing his own objectives. We can see that Mark was interested in Louise's supervisory style. Mark built trust with Louise when he said, "Being tested like that would have bothered me, too." Here Mark not only sprinkled a little information about himself into the interview, but he also established a connection with Louise. He said to her, "I know exactly what you're talking about because I would have felt as you did." He did it in a way that really meant he heard her. If he had said, "I understand what you mean," that would have told her nothing. We'll talk more about intentional listening and how to use those skills in Chapters 8 and 9.

TIPS TO BREAK DOWN BARRIERS AND CREATE TRUST IN THE INTERVIEW

Psychological Challenges Interviewers Encounter

Candidates walk into your office as strangers. You know little about them, and they know even less about you. During a very brief period of time you exert pressure on yourself to learn hidden information from the candidate. What is the likelihood of the candidate sharing hidden information with you? What is the likelihood of either of you sharing blind spots with each other?

To make matters worse, your goals and the candidates' goals differ. You are looking for someone to fill a vacant position and to successfully perform certain responsibilities in that job; they are looking for a means to provide income and benefits and certain psychological rewards that come with landing your job. Understanding how those goals interconnect takes a willingness to verbalize the real goals. *Most candidates prefer to answer your questions as they think you want them answered.* They prefer not to tell you their honest goals. For example, few candidates would tell you, "I'm looking for a high-paying job," or "I'm looking for any job. I don't care what I do." They prefer to keep that information hidden. You, too, prefer to keep certain aspects about the job hidden, for example, "This job is deadly dull," or "Your potential boss is a tyrant." Few interviewers tell candidates everything about the job and company—there are certain things they prefer to keep "inside."

Because you and the candidate don't know each other and you share different goals, how do you know when the candidate is being open and honest? Skillful candidates know how to appear sincere while they continue to hold their hidden information tucked away. Most of us don't even know when our friends or family are honest with us; being able to discover when a stranger is honest presents a much more formidable challenge.

With these psychological challenges in mind, let's look at some ways you can break down barriers.

- Keep the beginning of the interview safe by sprinkling in information about yourself and the job.
- Notice nonverbal cues that tell you what might be going on with the person; for example, if the candidate leans back in the chair, uncrosses legs, smiles often, gives you eye contact, or asks questions.
- Once into the interview, use the intentional listening skill of reflection to strengthen trust. The point of a reflection is to mirror feelings. You don't want to overuse this skill, but you want to use it enough to close the gap between you and the candidate. Mark said, "Wow, I bet that made you proud!" This is an example of a skillfully used reflection.

- Use the person's first name often and encourage her to use your first name. This can be done in the introductions. "My name is Mark Basin. Please call me Mark. May I call you Louise?" Don't assume a first-name basis. This small request shows respect.

- If you plan to take notes in an interview—which I would encourage you *not* to do—say something like, "I have one of those memories like a sieve. I need to jot down a few notes. I hope that's okay with you." Bear in mind that note taking increases the likelihood of defensiveness and will make building trust more difficult. Doing so also risks missing vital nonverbal cues. Nonetheless, if you must take notes, you must, but make sure your note taking is minimal. You do not need to write down every word. (I do, however, encourage you to write down everything you remember from the interview directly *after* the interview. If you wait until later in the day, you will forget!)

- If the candidate asks you a question, do everything you can to answer it. In other words, do not hedge or appear to hide something. If we expect candidates to share information from their hidden area, we must do so as well (or appear to do so). For example, imagine the boss in the job you are trying to fill is a known tyrant and the candidate asks you, "What is your honest assessment of the man I'd be working for?" Here are some approaches: (1) Be honest. Remember you want to hire smart and keep 'em. If we are dishonest here and say something like, "He's a wonderful boss, always there for his people," and the reverse is true, that new employee will not last. (2) Do not share everything. You can be honest without giving too much detail. Avoid adding your subjective judgment. Only share facts. (3) Describe the person's behaviors. Don't use highly charged words like *tyrant*. All of us have a different view of what a tyrant looks like. You want to be clear in your response, not fuzzy. Let's look at a response to that question: "I wish you had not asked me that question, but since you have, I will be honest. We have had complaints about the way Jeff micromanages. But I'm sure with your knowledge and experience, his attention to detail will not pose a problem for you." Your response is honest without giving too much detail, and the candidate can decide if she wants to work for a micromanager.

- Be open yourself. You come into the interview knowing much more about the candidate than he knows about you. You have the benefit of a résumé in front of you. What does he have? Sprinkle little bits about yourself throughout the interview—not all at once. You wouldn't want to give a long description of your past experiences. In the short clip of an interview we observed with Mark and Louise, what do we know about Mark? He works in acquisitions, and he travelled to France while in college. My guess is we'll learn more about him as the interview progresses.

- Spend the first few minutes of the interview exploring an icebreaker rather than digging into one of your target competencies.

WHAT IS AN ICEBREAKER?

Icebreakers do exactly what the name suggests: they break down the barriers that surround us. Icebreakers help us chip away at those psychological walls and open the Johari window. Many action-oriented managers ignore icebreakers, wanting to get to the meat of the interview right away. If the candidate left something off his résumé, these managers jump in with "So, what did you do after you stopped working for Sanders Company?" *Developing trust means taking the time to get to know the person. Icebreakers are the interviewer's tool to do that.* If you tend to be one of those managers who dislike icebreakers, think about selecting an icebreaker that relates to one of your target competencies. For example, when exploring team work, start the interview with questions pertaining to team sports. You learn a lot about a person's approach to teams as you keep the interview on safe ground. In reality, if you skip the icebreaker and jump full steam into the interview, the candidate will never open up to you. You will never accomplish the fundamental goal of a strategic interview. You will only discover the surface items the candidate wishes you to discover.

In some of my interviewing workshops, people tell me with pride how they enjoy stressing out a candidates during interviews. Some managers believe that the more stress a candidate experiences in an interview, the truer the picture of that person they'll see. Understanding the Johari window helps us see that this is an erroneous idea. The more stress a candidate feels, the more she will pull away. The goal of the strategic interview is not to add stress but to create openness, and that is a lot harder. Anyone can increase the stress in the already stressful interview environment. But only a highly skilled interviewer can create openness and trust.

Tips for Icebreakers

- Reveal something about yourself as part of the icebreaker. Notice how Mark said, "I spent 10 days in Paris after college. . . . " He didn't simply say, "What was it like being in France?" The small amount of self-disclosure helps the candidate open up and sets the tone for the interview. You could simply say something like, "I never had a chance to play team sports in college; what was it like being on the basketball team?" As you work on creating good, solid icebreakers, you'll notice that each icebreaker differs for each candidate. Just like with everything else in the strategic interview, you tailor your icebreaker to your candidate.

- Icebreakers are give and take. They do not necessarily feel like an interview. Interviews are nearly always questions and answers, back and forth. Icebreakers are comments, questions, responses—a conversation.

- Icebreakers never last more than a few minutes (otherwise you have a laissez-faire interview). After those initial minutes, transition from the icebreaker to key questions. You might say something like, "I've enjoyed learning more about your dancing experience, but now let's talk about your work with. . . . "

WHAT DO YOU TALK ABOUT DURING THE ICEBREAKER?

In most cases you can find something on the résumé that you can relate to, something similar to yourself. Perhaps the person is from the same area of the country as you are, attended the same university, or enjoys the same hobby. In some cases, however, you cannot spot anything on the résumé to talk about. In those cases, try one of the following:

• Talk about a current sports event that's on everyone's mind: "Wasn't the Ryder's Cup exciting? I don't play golf, but I couldn't help but get hooked on watching the Americans come from behind. That was teamwork at its best." Or, "Being from New York, I suspect you're following the World Series. My Southern roots put me on the side of the Braves. But either way, they are both outstanding teams."

• If the candidate looks totally unsportslike, you might talk about current weather-related news, such as the approach of a hurricane or flooding or extreme heat or cold. If the weather is perfectly gorgeous, you might say, "Don't you love days like this? When I look out my window and see the mountains framed in that sunshine and blue sky, it reminds me why I live in Colorado." This icebreaker might focus the early part of the interview on location preferences.

• If there are no sports or weather issues, you might start with a general, easy-to-answer question that gets you into the interview but also shares something about yourself. For example, "I'm curious about how you found out about our company. When I came here five years ago, there was no information out there. I had to really scratch to learn the basics."

Essentially, in an icebreaker you are searching for something safe to talk about that enables you to share a bit of information about yourself.

Interview the Whole Person

In the introduction to this book, we talked about the importance of interviewing the whole person. Openness in the interview and finding the perfect icebreaker is a good place for you to accomplish that task. To hire smart and keep 'em you want to interview beyond the work person; otherwise you may very well hire an excellent teacher or engineer but not someone who relates well with others. Often the résumé won't help you learn about the whole person. Some people omit their hobbies or outside interests. Although we want to hire productive people who will give us more than a nine-to-five attention span, we do not want a pure workaholic.

Well-rounded people have many interests. Work and work-related activities comprise a part of those interests. If you see nothing on the résumé to give you a clue about the whole person, simply ask, "What do you enjoy doing outside of work?" This question helps you determine if outside interests exist that the candidate simply left off the résumé. One caution, however: this question could lead you into some high-risk areas. The candidate might say something like, "As a single mom, I have little time for more than dealing with my kids and my work." If you get that response, leave it. You may uncover more outside interests as you proceed into the interview.

If, however, you learn that the person enjoys hunting or golf or Saturday morning pick-up basketball, you can use that information to create a nice icebreaker.

ICEBREAKER EXAMPLES

The icebreaker begins right after the initial introductions, often once the candidate has a seat.

Example 1

Interviewer: You and I are fellow Rotarians. How long have you been a member?

Candidate: I joined in the mid-90s and have thoroughly enjoyed it.

Interviewer: Me, too. We have a strong Rotary Club here. I go nearly every week. And, last month, I was the speaker. It was nice to be able to tell my fellow Rotarians about my work here.

Candidate: I spoke to the group last year. I was a nervous wreck, but everyone was so supportive. One of the things I really like about the club is the way people help each other, and, of course, the club supports a lot of the local charities.

Interviewer: Speaking of charities, you've worked for quite a few nonprofits. What was it like working in a nonprofit versus a profit environment?

Example 2

Interviewer: Thanks for coming in to see us on this awful rainy day. I left in the morning without an umbrella. I thought I would drown.

Candidate: Fortunately, I paid attention to the weather report and grabbed all my rain gear before leaving the house.

Interviewer: We've needed rain. This summer we've had less rain than ever; we've broken all the records. My garden just about dried up. But once the rain started, it's like a monsoon, and all my tomato plants rotted. Does it rain this much in Connecticut?

Candidate: We've had less rain than usual too in New Haven, but I don't think it's been as serious as it has here. We've been lucky.

Interviewer: The climate is just one difference living on this side of the country compared to the East Coast. My guess is you've experienced a number of things. What makes you want to return to the Southwest?

Both these examples are short. The first exemplifies a situation where the interviewer noticed something on the résumé he could talk about with the candidate; the second illustrates a situation where the interviewer couldn't find anything to relate to on the résumé.

In this chapter we examined the importance of keeping the interview open, the O in the POINT process. When interviewers create trust in the interview, they are more likely to learn something the candidate did not intend for them to learn—information from the hidden area. We explored the Johari window in relation to human interaction and the interview environment. Then we looked at ways strategic interviewers can keep interviews open by sprinkling information about themselves and by using icebreakers. A skillful interviewer understands how difficult it is to create trust and works hard to make that happen.

Effective use of the intentional listening skills will also enable interviewers to create and build trust. In Chapter 7 we will begin a thorough examination of how to listen with intentionality in order to hire smart and keep 'em.

PRACTICE EXERCISE: CREATE THE PERFECT ICEBREAKER

Answer *True* or *False* to the following questions.

1. Icebreakers are only useful for candidates who appear really nervous.
2. If you come across a good icebreaker, you should use it with every candidate.
3. Talking about the weather is a good way to break the ice.
4. Most people don't want to spend time talking about their hobbies. They want to get right into the interview.
5. An icebreaker should last at least 15 minutes for it to be effective.

See Appendix A for answers.

SEVEN

Listen with Intentionality

In the last chapter we explored trust and openness, the O in the POINT process. So far we've looked at the P (plan) and the O (open). This chapter initiates an in-depth study of the *IN: intentional listening*. The fact that the IN resides in the center of the word POINT signals its importance. *Intentional listening is the core of interviewing*. Even so, few books on the market deal with listening while discussing interviewing. They are more concerned with the mechanics of recruiting (screening résumés, selecting candidates, making decisions). It continues to amaze me that the actual interview gets lost in the process, and intentional listening barely makes the top of the list. In the late 1990s when I began looking at the literature, I found one book that dealt with listening in the interview. Martin Yate discussed layered listening in his book *Hiring the Best: a Manager's Guide to Effective Interviewing*.[1] In this chapter we will look at how layered listening fits with the intentional listening skills.

Today more books mention listening, but in small doses. For instance, we would expect to see more on listening from psychiatrist Mornell, but he devoted one page to listening in his 200-plus page book. There he told us "to listen carefully." Unfortunately he shared little about *how* to listen carefully. The most poignant example he gave us was how to use silence.[2]

Because listening is the foundation of all communication, particularly that required for an interview, we will spend the next three chapters on the subject. We will look at what intentional listening is and how it affects the interview. We will define the six intentional listening skills and learn when to use each as part of your interview strategy. We will explore examples of interviews where listening forms the core response on the part of the interviewer.

WHAT DOES INTENTIONAL LISTENING MEAN?

I once heard someone say, "I don't get intentional listening. Isn't all listening intentional?" Unfortunately, no. Most listening—the majority of listening—is passive listening. Your mother probably scolded you, saying, "What I tell you goes in one ear and out the other." She described passive listening.

Carl Rogers coined the term *active listening* and for the first time described a kind of listening that is more than passive listening. He trained psychologists and other therapists to employ active listening while interviewing patients. Imagine for a moment how a psychologist learns what is going on with a patient. She does not have the benefit of expensive testing, as does a medical doctor, nor can she observe the patient in action. Instead she must use her strong listening skills to hear more than the words. That was what Rogers taught his students when he taught active listening.

Intentional listening is similar to active listening in that it requires you to do more than simply sit back and passively listen. You must do something with what you hear. Unlike active listening, it does not delve into the subconscious (the unknown area). *What you want to do with intentional listening is listen with a purpose or an intent.* The intent or purpose relates to your target competencies. In other words, you listen for those competencies, like a miner searching for nuggets of gold, and dig in those places to unearth bits of information that will help you decide to hire or not.

How Intentional Listening Works

The process of intentional listening is quite simple. What you do is *hear what the person says, react, and then give feedback.* Olson gave us the foundation for this concept when he created one of the first interviewing processes in the literature: to listen, restate, and give feedback.[3] I've taken Olson's notion and expanded it to give you a clearer picture of how to restate. In other words, there is more to listening than simply restating what the person said as illustrated in Figure 7.1 which shows what intentional listening looks like.

Let's examine how intentional listening works with some examples.

Interviewer: Tell me how you learned about our company.

Candidate: I was looking for a progressive company in our area that dealt with modern concepts related to biotechnology. When I looked online, I found a number of interesting places in the greater Chicago area. I narrowed my search by looking for those that have been in existence for no more than 10 years, knowing the more mature companies may be a bit too bureaucratic for my taste. But I did want a company that had been around longer than just a few years. I wanted some stability. Mason's Research popped up. I looked over your annual reports and research findings. I was impressed.

Figure 7.1   The process of Intentional Listening

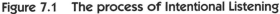

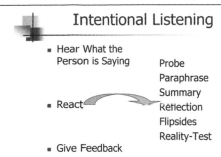

Intentional Listening

- Hear What the
  Person is Saying   Probe
                            Paraphrase
                            Summary
- React   Reflection
                            Flipsides
                            Reality-Test
- Give Feedback

Interviewer: That sounds like a great analysis. Tell me what you are looking for in a career with us.

This interviewer asked a nice probe, "Tell me how you learned about our company." The candidate described at length how he researched the company. In the process of talking about what he did, the interviewer got a good idea of the kind of company this candidate was seeking. But did the interviewer *hear what the candidate said*? The interviewer's response, "That sounds like a great analysis. Tell me what you are looking for in a career," was not a reaction by our definition of intentional listening. The interviewer gave feedback without reacting. In this example the candidate had no idea if he was heard of not.

Let's redo this interview with an intentional listening response.

Interviewer: Tell me how you learned about our company.
Candidate: I was looking for a progressive company in our area that dealt with modern concepts related to biotechnology. When I looked online, I found a number of interesting places in the greater Chicago area. I narrowed my search by looking for those that have been in existence for no more than 10 years, knowing the more mature companies may be a bit too bureaucratic for my taste. But I did want a company that had been around longer than just a few years. I wanted some stability. Mason's Research popped up. I looked over your annual reports and research findings, I was impressed.
Interviewer: When you say "not too bureaucratic for your taste," what do you mean?
Candidate: I've worked in large labs where we get so bogged down with paperwork we lose focus on what we're all about. Often the research takes a back seat to the bureaucratic red tape.
Interviewer: So you do not like a lot of paperwork?

Candidate: I realize that paperwork is necessary, especially when the project is grant funded, but I suppose I do resent having to do so much that I feel I can't do my job.

Interviewer: I know exactly what you're talking about with getting drowned in paperwork. We all find that frustrating. How have you handled it when you encountered those kinds of situations?

Candidate: I do the paperwork and carry on. Whenever I work with a federally funded grant, that's going to be the case, and I recognize that. What annoys me more is when the company adds paperwork that isn't necessary. In my last job, I spoke to the head of the department. We managed to eliminate a lot of unnecessary paperwork, and it made all our jobs easier.

Interviewer: So you and your supervisor managed to get rid of some of the red tape that the company—not the grant—required. That must have been quite rewarding for you.

Notice how much more this interviewer learned by reacting to what the candidate said before finally giving feedback. In this scenario we do not wonder if the interviewer heard what the candidate said. It is clear that the interviewer not only heard but also heard with intent. He picked out a particular point and probed from there. That's what intentional listening is all about. The interviewer might have selected other points to probe; for example, "So tell me what you mean when you say you're looking for a progressive company," or "You say you want stability in a company; help me understand why that is important to you." *Listening with intent means listening for your target competencies and reacting.*

COMMUNICATION DEFINED

Communication is behavior that transmits meaning from one person to another person.[4]

This definition tells you that you cannot communicate without *doing something*. It also tells you that communication does not happen unless *meaning* is transmitted. Of course what I mean and what you think I mean pose another challenge. In fact, I can name at least six messages in any conversation:

- What you *mean* to say
- What you *actually* say
- What the other person *hears*
- What the other person *thinks* she hears
- What the other person *says*
- What you *think* the other person says.[5]

To complicate matters, your mind thinks *four* times faster than the average person can speak. Even when you *try* to listen, your thinking mind flies many miles an hour in another direction. Harnessing all that thinking energy takes discipline, focus, and concentration. In today's world, where most of us multitask our way through life, stopping to really hear another person seems daunting. As you communicate in the interview, you will see how important it is to stop doing whatever it is you are doing, to set your antenna in the direction of the speaker, and to assign your thinking mind the job of listening.

Active listening, as Rogers described it, gives the listener no rest. In various studies into the physical response of an active listener, Rogers learned that blood pressure rose and heartbeat increased during the act of listening. In other words, active listening takes a lot of physical energy. Although intentional listening is not as extreme as active listening (because we're not trying to unearth what's in the subconscious), it still takes energy. After a day of interviewing, you should feel physically tired.

WHY IS LISTENING SO HARD?

Listening is the foundation for communication. If you do not listen, you do not communicate. Yet whose life is not fraught with instances where we either do not listen or others do not listen to us? Besides the physical exertion of it, what makes listening so hard?

- You assume in advance what the speaker is about to say is uninteresting or unimportant or you've heard it before. After you've interviewed (particularly in the screening process) 10 or 12 candidates, you begin to think that you will hear the same old story over and over. This assumption shuts listening down. For example, when an interviewer asks, "Tell me what made you select our company," most candidates say something like, "Because it is such a well-respected company in the industry." But let's say a candidate says instead, "I really don't know much about your company and was curious to see what you had to offer." If you miss that comment, you've lost a chance to dig deeper in order to learn this candidate's motivation for looking at your company.

- You start to formulate your next question. Once in an interview workshop, I stopped an interviewer right in the middle and asked, "What did the candidate just say?" The interviewer had no idea because she was formulating her next question. This is a common mistake and one all interviewers struggle to avoid.

- You mentally criticize the speaker's delivery. If the candidate slurs his response or if he speaks too slowly or too quickly, you may miss what he said. This is one of the most difficult barriers to avoid because once a candidate says something in a way that troubles you, it is hard to stop your mind from mentally criticizing and thereby missing what was said. It happens, and when it does, just move on and try to avoid it happening again.

- You disagree with something the speaker said and begin to formulate your rebuttal. In an interview you often do not verbally refute a candidate's viewpoint, but you may mentally do so, and when you do, once again, you miss the point the candidate may have been trying to make, and the opportunity to follow up with an intentional listening skill vanishes.

- You hear only the factual data and tune out the rest. Some interviewers do not give credence to emotional content. They focus on facts alone. Facts give us some data, but the nonverbal cues, which carry the emotional data, give you the in-depth information you'll need if you want to explore deeper. This is especially true in an interview where candidates are trying to keep things in their hidden area. For example, the interviewer asks, "What happened in your current job to make you decide to leave?" The candidate responds, "I have been in that job for over 10 years. I've enjoyed the work and the people. But things changed in the last six months, and I realized that for me to advance, I needed to look elsewhere." (The candidate says this with eyes downcast. When she says "things changed," she takes a deep, tired-sounding breath.) This candidate's response suggests issues that really disappointed her. If the interviewer misses these cues, he will miss a vital area in which to probe.

- You tune out certain words, expressions, or phrases. If you are offended by certain words or expressions, you might tune out the rest of the candidate's response.

- You jump to conclusions, right or wrong. This again is a difficult barrier to avoid. Once you have interviewed multiple candidates, you are more likely to jump to conclusions. Perceptions play a key role here. If you notice yourself jumping to conclusions a lot, you may be susceptible to the eroding influence of perceptions.

- Your mind simply wanders. As we said earlier, your mind thinks four times faster than the average person can speak. During any interaction, it is impossible to completely harness that wandering mind. Your goal is to recognize this problem and channel that energy to listening. When your mind wanders during an interview, the best thing to do is to admit it and ask the candidate to repeat what she just said.

When you react to what a candidate said (using the intentional listening skills), you tell the candidate you're listening and you set up opportunities for strategic questions. You cannot react if you fall prey to any of the above barriers. I've had people in my workshops protest, "I did hear what the candidate said, but I just didn't react." The reality is if you don't react, you *appear as if* you didn't hear.

In real life, it's hard to hear everything someone says, and you will find yourself tuning out no matter how hard you try. When that happens (hopefully not frequently), you must move on and strive not to let it happen again. In other words, you definitely want to react when you've heard and save your "nonreactions" for those few times when you couldn't control your wandering mind.

In essence, as a strategic interviewer you use one of the six intentional listening skills to react to what candidates say. You do not react to everything a candidate says but only those things that relate to your target competencies. If, for example, a candidate tells you about her recent promotion, you listen politely (passively). When she says, "My boss thought I had the flexibility to perform well as a project manager," you perk up because flexibility is one of your target competencies, and you say, "Give me an example of when you showed flexibility on the job."

SIX INTENTIONAL LISTENING SKILLS

Let's discuss the six intentional listening skills listed in the introductory chapter to this book in greater detail.

WHAT ARE THE INTENTIONAL LISTENING SKILLS AND WHEN ARE THEY USED?

Probe	An open question that seeks to find out more information about something. Probes search for information when that information is vague or unspecific.
Paraphrase	A statement that rephrases in another person's words what the person just said. Paraphrases seek to clarify what was said or to search for a deeper understanding, and they have an understood question mark at the end of them.
Summary	A series of paraphrases that summarize what was said. The purpose of a summary statement is to consolidate a large amount of information.
Reality Tests	A series of probes and paraphrases designed to test the reality of what was said.
Flipside	A probe that forces the person to share the opposite point of view.
Reflection	A statement that requires you to reflect (as in a mirror) the feelings you hear behind the words being expressed. Often your sense of the feeling comes from the person's nonverbal cues.

Probe

For interviewing purposes, the probe is the most important intentional listening skill. By "probe" we mean an open question (see definition in Chapter 2) that digs deeper. Probes piggy-back what was previously said. Chapter 8 will provide more examples of probes and when to use a probe in an interview. The following is an example of a probe.

Candidate: I'm interested in finding a job that requires me to use my skills as a social worker. I spent four years in college and hope to put those skills to work.

Interviewer: When you say "use your skills," what exactly do you mean?

This probe piggy-backs, or layers—to use Yate's term—what was previously said. By layering your probes you show the listener that you heard what he said. If you do not layer, you might say, for example, "Describe what you did in your last job." This is a perfectly good probe, but it does not piggy-back what the candidate said, and it leaves the candidate wondering if the interviewer heard what was said.

As a strategic interviewer, you will opt to piggy-back your probes in every instance *except* the following:

• The previous statement touches on a high-risk legal area.

• You've already covered the areas mentioned. In other words, you've dug as deeply as you need to.

• The area mentioned by the candidate does not touch on target competencies for which you are exploring. (Perhaps another interviewer is exploring that area or it is not a target competency for that particular job.)

Paraphrase

As an interviewer you will use paraphrasing almost as much as you use the probe. It is the second most important intentional listening skill. Paraphrases seek to clarify what the candidate previously said. They show the candidate you heard what she said and want to know more. They give the candidate a chance to clarify and talk more about a topic. When there is nothing left to say, the candidate merely acknowledges what you said. Besides the clarifying function, paraphrases also give the candidate a break. Too many probes feel like an interrogation. The following is an example of a paraphrase.

Candidate: When I worked for the Athletic Association, I had an opportunity to go to all the home games. I felt as though I was part of something bigger than simply typing and filing. We all

were a part of the team. When the team won, everyone
celebrated together as if we all had a part in it.

Interviewer: It sounds as if you like working in a job where there is a
strong team spirit.

Candidate: I do. In fact, in my last job, we didn't have much team spirit. I
started a pick-up basketball game on Saturday mornings.
Most everyone participated and it was great fun. Before long
we grew closer as a work team

This paraphrase not only resulted in clarification from the candidate but
also produced more information for the interviewer to explore.

Flipside

Because candidates want you to see the rosy side of every situation, it is
often hard to determine if everything is as rosy as the candidate says. Could
there be a flipside? The goal of flipside is to explore the other side of the coin;
otherwise, candidates allow you to only see them at their best. Clearly, candidates try to keep their worst sides hidden, but your job as a strategic interviewer is to uncover both the positive and the negative. Chapter 8 will
explore the use of flipsides with examples in an interview environment. The
following is an example of an interviewer using flipside to get beyond the
rosy superficialities.

Candidate: My boss was very easy to work for. I enjoyed the opportunity
to learn from her. She'd been with the company for a long
time and knew all the ins and outs. Because I was younger,
she took me under her wing. I became her right-hand assistant and learned a lot about how to operate a large corpora-
tion. I would have never had that opportunity with anyone
else.

Interviewer: It sounds as if your boss served as a mentor to you?

Candidate: That's right, and a perfect example. She taught me how to deal
with really hard situations, always to be fair but firm—that sort
of thing. It's what I hope to take to my next job.

Interviewer: I've had mentors in my career as well. Even though they
teach us a lot, there are some instances where their approach
might not be the best. Give me an example of when you and
your boss disagreed.

Notice how the interviewer began with a paraphrase and then followed up
with a flipside. She could have used the flipside directly after the description
of the boss, but she decided to paraphrase first to help determine what to flip.
Sometimes the candidate gives you so much rosy information it's hard to

identify which particular point you want to explore deeper. Try paraphrasing first and then follow with a flipside.

Summary

Although interviewers use the summary less frequently than the flipside, it is still a critical intentional listening skill. Summaries help the interviewer narrow the focus. Summarizing also gives the interviewer time to think before exploring another area. Chapter 9 will explore the uses of the summary and show examples of summaries in an interview environment. The following is one short example of a summary.

Candidate: When I worked on the project team, we split up duties and pulled together as a team in a way I've never seen happen before. In fact, I've worked on many teams, but this one was the most productive of my career. Other teams seem to falter and collapse if you're not careful. But the people on this team were really committed to the task. Everyone pulled together even when the going got tough. Once when we took our recommendations to the vice president and he nixed everything, we all felt pretty depressed at first, but it didn't last. We quickly regrouped and actually recognized that the ideas that the vice president had were good and might even strengthen the end product. As it turned out, we won the company's gold medal for the best project result. I was proud to be part of that team.

Interviewer: Let me see if I can summarize your evaluation of that team. You feel it was a highly effective team because the people were committed and looked for creative solutions when their ideas were challenged?

Notice how the interviewer collapsed a lot of information, pulling out the nuggets from a long description. From this summary, the interviewer can see how to regroup and where to redirect the interview.

Reality Test

The reality test is one of the most difficult intentional listening skills to put into practice. As far as interviewing goes, it is one of the least used. Nonetheless, it is one you may sometimes need. The point of a reality test is to show a candidate you cannot be snowed. You basically say to the candidate, "Now, what's that you say? Are you sure you mean that?" The Johari window taught us not to challenge a candidate early in the interview (even if the occasion arises). The reality test, therefore, is an effective tool later in the interview after you've created trust. Chapter 9 will show you examples of reality testing in an interview environment. The following is an example of a reality test.

Candidate:	I tend to be an outgoing person who loves people. I could spend my entire day interacting with people and never do anything else.
Interviewer:	You told me a few minutes ago that you enjoy getting to the office early when everything is quiet. Help me understand how you could enjoy spending your entire day dealing with people without a break.

The interviewer took an extreme statement—"I could spend my entire day interacting with people"—and tested the reality of it. Reality tests could appear to be sarcastic if not carefully worded. You don't want to imply you don't believe what she said. Instead you want to say, "tell me what you really mean without using extremes."

Reflection

If you were one of Carl Rogers's psychology trainees, you would use reflection often. In fact, reflection would be your number one intentional listening skill. But for interviewing purposes, reflections fall further down the priority line. Nonetheless, an opportunity for a reflection could surface at least once in *most* interviews. The point of a reflection is to mirror back a feeling you pick up through the nonverbal cues. Chapter 9 will demonstrate reflection in an interview environment. The following example shows you what a reflection looks like.

Candidate:	My last job seemed like it would be really interesting. When I took the job I expected to work with the design of products, particularly using the new graphics programs we used at Seminole when I worked there. But as soon as I was hired, I realized the company was way behind the eight-ball graphically. And they were not interested in upgrading their systems.
Interviewer:	It sounds as though you were surprised by the company's lack of computer sophistication and somewhat disappointed.

The point of a reflection is to really hear the feelings behind the words. This interviewer identified two feelings: surprise and disappointment.

INTENTIONAL LISTENING SKILLS IN AN INTERVIEW

We've defined the six intentional listening skills (the way we put listening into action) and seen each in a brief example. Let's examine an interview where the interviewer uses all six skills.

Interviewer: Thank you for interviewing with our company. My name is Mary Johnson. I manage the process engineering division. Please make yourself comfortable. May I call you Jeff? (Candidate sits down.)

Jeff: Sure. That's fine.

Mary: I noticed on your résumé that you worked as a golf assistant in Smallsville for three summers. What other work experiences have you had? (probe)

Jeff: I haven't had any real work experiences yet. I worked as an intern during my senior year at Billings Company, but that was just a few hours a week.

Mary: Tell me, Jeff, what did you do in that intern position? (probe)

Jeff: Mostly, I did clerical stuff. I ran copies and made charts on the computer. Sometimes I ran errands for them. (Responds with brisk, short responses.)

Mary: So you didn't use any of your chemical engineering experience? (paraphrase)

Jeff: When I went there, I thought I'd be learning more about chemical engineering practice, but they really didn't let me do much. I did sit in on their team meetings a couple of times. That was a real experience. (Rolls his eyes upward)

Mary: (Sits forward) You seem frustrated with the nature of that intern experience. (reflection)

Jeff: You could put it that way. My friends got better positions. Some even got to co-op for the summer at one company, and they really learned the ropes. Because I had to earn as much as possible to pay for my education, I had to return home. I earned twice as much on the golf course.

Mary: I, too, had to work my way through school. It's not easy. Tell me what you learned during your internship. (probe)

Jeff: (Sits up and gives the interviewer direct eye contact) For one thing, most companies don't put much stress on creativity. I noticed in the team meetings that everyone just went along with each other. Nobody challenged the team leader's ideas or direction.

Mary: How did you act during those meetings? (probe)

Jeff: (Sits back in his seat and breaks the eye contact) Of course I was in no position to challenge anyone. Why would they listen even if I did? Mostly I just did as I was told. But I thought the meetings were a big waste of time.

Mary: So you didn't do anything or say anything to anyone about your feelings about the team meetings? (reality test)

Jeff: No. I suppose I could've said something to Dr. Matthews. He got the internship for me. But, well, what would be the point anyway? There wasn't anything he could do either.

Mary: Tell me about meetings you've been in where you didn't feel they were a waste of time. (flipside)

Jeff: At the club where I worked during the summer, we had staff meetings. I really liked the golf pro. He listened to everyone's ideas and often made changes that people suggested.

Mary: I'm getting the impression that you like working for people who listen to your ideas. (paraphrase)

Jeff: Yeah, particularly when the boss pays attention and actually does what we suggest.

Mary: Give me an example of a time when you suggested a change during one of those meetings. (probe)

Jeff: They had this system with the golf carts. People signed out carts by hand and then the guy in the shop put down the member's name and number. It was cumbersome, and often they didn't record the right name. I suggested we put the stuff on the computer and train everyone to enter the data. This was a small, private club, and they didn't have much computer sense. Anyway, that summer I helped them automate their system.

Mary: That sounds like something you're proud of. (reflection)

Jeff: (Smiles) I guess so. But when people listen to your ideas, it's easy to make suggestions. I found out in that internship that when people don't listen, I tend to be quiet.

Mary: So it sounds like you learned something about yourself even if you didn't gain the chemE knowledge you might have hoped for? (summary)

In this example we saw Mary use every intentional listening skill to help Jeff clarify, open up, and share information he may not have intended to share. If Mary had used probes and nothing else, Jeff may have shut down. He seemed reserved at the beginning of the interview (as are most candidates). By the end of the interview, particularly after Mary used two reflections, he opened up and shared his view of teams and team leaders.

DON'T OVERDO IT

One final note regarding the Intentional listening skills: too much of a good thing won't work. In other words, interviewers must skillfully use probes, paraphrases, summaries, reality tests, flipsides, and reflections. Imagine how frustrating it would be if the interviewer only paraphrased or only reflected, and you already know that too many probes feels like a cross-examination. Interviewers must balance the responses in order to uncover the most information.

Chapters 8 and 9 will help you more thoroughly understand these vital skills and when to use them. The more comfortable you get with each intentional listening skill, the better able you'll be to balance the interview and use the most appropriate skill strategically.

ASSESS YOURSELF: DO YOU LISTEN WITH INTENT?

1. If someone says something that I don't understand, I can
   a. ask them to repeat themselves.
   b. paraphrase back what they said.
   c. ignore it and move on.

2. When I use a probe, I often start it with
   a. "Could you tell me. . . ."
   b. "Describe a situation. . . ."
   c. "Did you do. . . ."

3. Reality tests are great to use
   a. late in the interview.
   b. never in an interview.
   c. when I can't think of anything else to say.

4. When a candidate gives you all the positive aspects of her last job, it's a good idea to
   a. give her positive feedback.
   b. move on to your next question.
   c. ask her to tell you the challenges she faced.

5. If your mind checks out during the interview, you should
   a. ask your next question about something totally different.
   b. admit you didn't hear what was said and apologize.
   c. paraphrase what you think you heard.

6. If your candidate talks a lot, you can
   a. ask lots of questions about what he said.
   b. summarize.
   c. interrupt and ask a closed question.

7. One way to react with intent to what a candidate says is to
   a. give feedback.
   b. use a flipside.
   c. smile.
8. When listening to someone, it's a good idea to
   a. prepare your rebuttal in your head.
   b. draw your conclusions as she speaks.
   c. reflect the feelings you see expressed.
9. In an interview when you can't think of anything else to say, you should
   a. summarize.
   b. end the interview.
   c. ask the candidate if he has any questions.
10. You probably do not want to piggy-back a candidate's answer when
   a. the candidate talked for too long.
   b. the candidate said something about her children.
   c. both a and b.
See Appendix A for answers.

EIGHT

Prominent Intentional Listening Skills: Probe, Paraphrase, and Flipside

In the last chapter we looked at the definition of intentional listening (IN in POINT), and we presented an overview of the six intentional listening skills. We saw that to perform a strategic interview you must listen with intent. Passive listening will not enable you to dig deeper. At the same time, if you try to react to everything a candidate says, you will lose focus. To create balance in a strategic interview requires you to listen but with a focus like a laser beam poised on a target.

This chapter will examine the prominent intentional listening skills: probe, paraphrase, and flipside. We will explore what to do when faced with vague situations. We will also clarify when to use which skill. Just like everything in a strategic interview, each intentional listening skill has a purpose. You would not use a flipside unless you had a reason to do so, always bearing in mind your ultimate goal: to get the candidate to tell you something she did not intend to tell you when she walked through the door.

THE PURPOSE OF PROBES AND HOW TO ASK THEM

As a strategic interviewer, you do not want to overuse any one of the intentional listening skill. As we've said earlier, if you probe too much the candidate will feel interrogated. Yet probes are the most used intentional listening skill in any interview. If you find yourself probing too much, consider your purpose. Are you trying to gain too much information too fast? Could you substitute another intentional listening skill in the place of the probe? *The reason you want to learn all the intentional listening skills and the purpose for each is to give your interview balance and to keep it flowing.*

When to Use a Probe

Use the probe when you want to find out more about something; that is, when you want to gain information.

In Chapter 4 we defined a probe as an open question designed to dig deeper for information. Probes by their very definition cannot be closed questions. Closed questions are not designed to dig deeper. Closed questions are designed to get specific facts or to shut down information. One of the biggest mistakes interviewers make is to ask closed questions disguised as open questions. To be more precise, they ask closed questions, but they want more information. Then they later wonder why the candidate didn't talk more. Look at this example.

Interviewer:	Did you enjoy your last job?
Candidate:	Yes, but I knew it was not a career opportunity for me.
Interviewer:	Are you looking for a career opportunity?
Candidate:	That would be ideal.

This candidate answered with more than a "yes" or "no." Because the interviewer asked closed questions, however, the candidate could have simply answered in the affirmative or the negative without elaboration.

Another common mistake interviewers make is to ask "could you" or "would you" questions. To illustrate, how would you, define this question as open or closed: "Would you tell me about your recent promotion?" If you answered "closed," you are correct. By asking "could you" or "would you" questions, you are psychologically saying to the candidate, "Don't tell me too much." As a strategic interviewer, you want to psychologically say to the candidate, "Tell me everything."

The following are common ways to ask probes:

- What . . .
- How . . .
- In what ways . . .
- Tell me . . .
- Describe for me . . .
- Give me an example . . .

We've omitted a number of question words, such as *where*, *when*, and *why*. There is nothing wrong with asking a "where" or "when" question, but they usually result in single-word answers. This is not always the case and varies depending on what you are seeking.

"Why" questions, on the other hand, cause problems. Let's look at what happens when an interviewer uses "why" questions.

Candidate: I'm really interested in finding a job where I can use my accounting skills.
Interviewer: Why do you want to use your accounting skills?
Candidate: Well, I spent four years in college learning how to be an accountant. I would like to put those skills to good use.
Interviewer: Why did you study accounting?
Candidate: I like working with numbers and accounting seemed like a good career where I could find a job.
Interviewer: Why didn't you get a job in accounting sooner?
Candidate: There weren't any available when I left college.

This candidate is answering the interviewer's questions, but we're getting a sense of defensiveness. When you use "why" questions, the natural response is to defend yourself or your choices. *In a strategic interview we do not want defensive people; we want open people.* Whenever possible, avoid "why" questions. Let's examine this same interview without the "why."

Candidate: I'm really interested in finding a job where I can use my accounting skills.
Interviewer: What is it that attracted you to accounting?
Candidate: I've always loved numbers, and while I was in school I was looking for a career where I could use numbers but also find a job when I got out. As soon as I took the first accounting course, I knew that was the place.
Interviewer: Tell me more about the specifics of accounting that you want to use in your next job.

By avoiding "why" probes, the interviewer kept the interview flowing. Already this interviewer learned much more about the candidate's career goals than the interviewer who probed with "whys."

The examples of probes in Table 8.1 show how to use a probe to gain more information from a vague response.

THE PURPOSE OF PARAPHRASES AND HOW TO ASK THEM

A paraphrase says what the candidate just said but in your own words. For example:

Candidate: My job with the insurance company meant I had to travel all over the state. It gave me a good opportunity to learn this state. I can probably name all 100 counties.

Table 8.1   Examples of Probe Responses

Candidate Response	Follow-Up Probe
I usually work on my own, but I like working on teams.	Tell me about the teams you've worked on.
During my internship we worked on a design project.	What exactly did you do on that project?
I believe it takes leadership to get people to work for you.	Give me a specific example of how you've shown that kind of leadership.

Interviewer: So you enjoyed traveling?

   Candidate: I enjoyed getting to know the state. The traveling and staying in small motels along the way was really rough.

In this case, the interviewer paraphrased for clarification, and the candidate corrected her, helping the interviewer learn more about what he meant. Had she not paraphrased, she may have thought the candidate liked traveling in his last job.

You might wonder about overuse of the paraphrase. Clearly probing and probing will eventually lead to a sense of violation, but what about paraphrases? Imagine overusing paraphrases, for example:

   Candidate: I worked directly with the chief operating officer in my last job, and that gave me a lot of opportunities. My job was varied and active. I loved that. I don't like sitting in front of my computer all day and never leaving my desk.

Interviewer: So you enjoy being busy?

   Candidate: Yes, in fact when I'm busy I'm most productive.

Interviewer: Being busy means you get more done?

   Candidate: Right.

So, now what? You couldn't very well paraphrase, "Right." The candidate shut down at the end of the series. Even two paraphrases in a row could dry up your responses. Just like with the probe, you must use the paraphrase when you have a strategic purpose, and you must be judicious. Paraphrases are the second most prominent intentional listening skill in your repertoire, but that doesn't mean you should overuse them. Years ago I knew a woman who paraphrased everything I said to her. At first I thought it odd and rather funny. It didn't matter what I said, she paraphrased it back. After a while I avoided her. The habit had become most annoying. When paraphrases are skillful, candidates don't even notice them. If they start to notice, you've paraphrased too much.

The Purpose of a Paraphrase

The most common purpose of a paraphrase is to clarify what you heard with the intent of gaining more information. In other words, *the paraphrase is not a statement but a question*. Even if the sentence ends in a period, your voice rises slightly to suggest a question mark. Otherwise, you end the conversation. At times you may wish to end the conversation. For example, when you come to the end of a series of questions, you paraphrase to bring the discussion to a conclusion. In that case, you would end with a downward intonation or a period. Normally, however, your goal is to clarify with the desire to go deeper.

Another purpose of a paraphrase is to break up your probes. If you've asked several probes in a row, you may want to stop, regroup, and toss in a paraphrase before you begin probing again. *Paraphrases are good rest stops*. They give you and the candidate a chance to take a breath. For example:

Interviewer:	What happened after you left your last job?
Candidate:	I began working at home. I developed a new business designed to help people find the best consultants. I was a consultant-middleperson, so to speak.
Interviewer:	How did you land in this niche?
Candidate:	(Laughs) That's a good question. Actually, when I worked for the state, we outsourced a lot of things. Our purpose was to find the lowest bidder, but that wasn't always the best choice. I learned that there was a lot more to choosing a good consulting firm than simply price. After my second baby, I knew I wanted to be at home more. I had colleagues where I worked who said they appreciated my ability to find great consultants. They didn't have the time to do the due diligence that I used to do. I started helping them out, and that sort of grew.
Interviewer:	It sounds like you had a special talent for finding good consulting teams?
Candidate:	Yes, I suppose I do. I have learned some things that help me match people. It's been fun.
Interviewer:	You say you worked from home. What was that like for you?
Candidate:	It's been a challenge. The problem is you work all the time; there are no breaks. I work weekends, holidays. I thought I'd have more time with my kids, but as it turns out I have less. Although the business is going well and I've learned a lot, I'm ready to move on to something steadier.
Interviewer:	What do you mean by "steadier"?

This interviewer asked some great probes (and was careful to avoid the high-risk area that could have been a problem). After the second probe, he threw in a paraphrase to break up the steady questioning: "Sounds like you have a special talent for finding good consulting teams?" This paraphrase not only kept the interview going, but it complimented the candidate.

If you are team interviewing, a paraphrase is a nice way to signal your partner that you are finished with that series of questions and ready for her to take over.

One of the biggest problems interviewers have with paraphrases is not listening. When your mind travels away, you cannot paraphrase. Be on the alert; if your mind wanders, do not try to paraphrase. If you miss the mark completely, you will lose the candidate's trust. Imagine, for example, this interviewer having said something like, "So you like working at home." Oops! The candidate would have likely thought, "Did I say that? I don't think so."

The following are some typical ways to initiate a paraphrase:

- In other words . . .
- If I hear you correctly . . .
- So . . . *or* So what you're saying is . . .
- Let me see if I understand . . .

Another tip is to avoid always using the same lead-in. If you say, "In other words" every time you paraphrase, it begins to sound forced. Just as you want to vary your intentional listening skills, you must also vary the way you approach those skills. You wouldn't want to start every probe with "What," and you wouldn't want to start every paraphrase with "In other words."

The examples of paraphrases in Table 8.2 show how to use a paraphrase to gain more information from a vague response.

THE PURPOSE OF FLIPSIDES AND HOW TO ASK THEM

We defined a flipside in the last chapter as a question that probes the other side of an issue. The purpose of a flipside is to reverse what you've heard. If

Table 8.2 Examples of Paraphrase Responses

Candidate Response	Follow-Up Paraphrase
I chose chemical engineering because I've always liked mixing things	So your interest in CE started when you were very young?
I couldn't decide on a major, so I ended up with a double in business.	In other words, choosing your major was a hard decision for you?
I worked at Pizza Hut part time when I was a freshman.	Am I clear, then, that you worked 20 hours a week while a full-time student your freshman year?

the candidate gives you an unbiased view of an issue—that is, if he tells you both sides—you need not employ a flipside. In an interview environment, candidates want you to hear about their strengths, not their weaknesses. They want you to believe that their experiences have been without conflict or tension. They want you to imagine that they've made all the right decisions and chosen the correct paths. For these reasons flipsides occur more frequently in an interview environment than they would in other instances. Nonetheless, if you are the parent of a teenager, you might experience many opportunities for flipsides as well. Doesn't your child want you to believe all her friends are A students or all the events she wants to attend are well chaperoned? Passive listening results in missing opportunities for flipsides. For example:

Candidate: Once I was promoted to lead salesman, I had five people under my direction. That was a great challenge. I had to not only meet my quotas, but I also had to help others reach theirs. I had the best team ever. We held frequent meetings to talk about how we could improve, and I loved the way everyone shared ideas. We brainstormed together, and people came up with the most creative suggestions. There was lots of laughter. Everyone supported each other even though we were all responsible for our individual territories and sales quotas.

Interviewer: That sounds like a great experience.

This interviewer blew it. She didn't flip what this candidate said and therefore only learned what the candidate wanted her to hear. For example, the candidate said they held frequent meetings. Often staff members deplore meetings. This candidate described the meetings as fun. What about when meetings are tense, not so fun? What about the people in the meetings who don't share their ideas, who quietly sit in the back? Was everyone laughing during these meetings?

Flipsides give the interviewer an opportunity to see into the hidden area, but in a gentle way. In this example the interviewer could have flipped any number of things, depending on her target competencies, for instance:

- "You say when you were promoted you had five people reporting to you. Being a new supervisor can be very difficult. What were some of the difficulties you faced with this new challenge?"
- "I love being in meetings when people are sharing lots of creative ideas, but I've also been in them where some people are quiet. Tell me how you handled bringing out the quiet participants."

- "Meetings can be very challenging as well as rewarding. You've talked about the rewards. Share some of the challenges you faced running these meeting with your sales team."
- "It sounds as though you had to deal with individual goals as well as team objectives. How did you balance the two?"

One mistake interviewers make with flipsides is to combine the two sides in one question. They ask something like, "Tell me about your strengths and your weaknesses as a supervisor." Whenever you combine two pieces of any probe, the candidate makes a choice to answer one more thoroughly than the other. It is much better to focus on one piece at a time and to drill down until you exhaust that line of inquiry before going to the next. Take a look at the following example:

Interviewer:	Tell me about your strengths as a team leader.
Candidate:	I'm a good listerner to other people's ideas. I'm also very energetic in teams, kind of like a cheerleader. When things don't go as well as we might have expected, I help the team bounce back.
Interviewer:	So you are a good listener and a good motivator, right?
Candidate:	Yes, and I'm also one who stays on task. I help the team keep focused.
Interviewer:	Give me an example when you had to help the team focus.

This interviewer could go on with several more questions, such as:

- "How do you know you're a good listener?"
- "Listening is great, but how do you handle the people who are less vocal in a team?"
- "Give me an example of how you helped the team bounce back from a bad situation."

Once this interviewer completes all these lines of questioning and any others that may relate to her target competencies, she is ready to ask the flipside question: "You've shared a lot about your strengths as a team leader; what about some of your weaknesses?"

The following are typical ways to begin a flipside.

- Thank you for sharing what you liked about ... What about some of the things you didn't enjoy as much?
- You seemed to enjoy ... Tell me what you found challenging.

- I'm impressed with everything you accomplished. What didn't you accomplish that you wish you had?
- Working with people is a great experience. Tell me about some of the challenges you faced . . .
- It's great when teams work harmoniously, but it's been my experience that good teams often go through conflict. How did you deal with the conflict your team experienced?
- Tell me about a conflict situation you had . . .

The examples of flipsides in Table 8.3 show how to use a flipside to gain more information from a one-sided response:

EXAMPLE OF AN INTERVIEW USING THE PROMINENT INTENTIONAL LISTENING SKILLS

Interviewer:	My name is Peter Davis. I'm the lead interviewer for our company and a project manager. Thank you for coming today to spend some time with us. I noticed that you and I both worked for Kroger while in college.
Candidate:	That's wild. I guess I shouldn't be too surprised. There were lots of us college kids working for Kroger when I was there. Did you work at the store on East Broad?
Interviewer:	(Laughs) Yes, actually. How was that experience for you—working for a grocery store, I mean? (probe)
Candidate:	I enjoyed it. The hours were rough. I worked from 3 p.m. to midnight. But I liked that we stayed busy. I moved up from bagboy to cashier in no time. The night-shift people were very nice and helped me learn the ropes.
Interviewer:	I remember those hours. I had to work the night shift a few times. Mostly I worked days. What other challenges

Table 8.3 Examples of Flipside Responses

One-Sided Response	Follow-Up Flipside
I love working with people.	What do you find challenging with working with people?
My boss and I get along really well.	Give me an example of what you did when you disagreed with your boss.
I've thoroughly enjoyed my college experience.	Tell me about a time when college felt overwhelming.

	did you face working for a store like Kroger? (flipside)
Candidate:	I suppose just feeling like you were not special. The chain was so big. I had a few ideas about ways to make the lines go smoother, but no one listened. They had to do what corporate wanted. In high school I worked in my dad's pharmacy. It wasn't a chain. There, I felt I had more say in what we did.
Interviewer:	In other words, you have trouble working in a big corporation where there are lots of layers? (paraphrase)
Candidate:	Back then I did, but I've gotten used to it. My first job out of college was with the Manning Corporation. They're based in New Jersey. We ran our division pretty independently, but my boss always worried about the guys in New Jersey.
Interviewer:	How did you learn to balance working independently but for a big corporation? (probe)
Candidate:	For one thing, I learned to keep my head down. I did my job, and didn't try to rock the boat. Right out of college we all think we have all the answers, but in reality those people in the trenches know a lot more than we ever thought about.
Interviewer:	When you say the people in the trenches know more, help me understand what you mean. (probe)
Candidate:	I mean those people with experience. I had a lot of book knowledge, but they knew the ropes. They knew which customers bought what and how much they'd be willing to spend. Nothing in the books taught me that. I learned to listen to them and to heed their tips.
Interviewer:	What about your book knowledge? How did you apply that to your first job? (probe)
Candidate:	Actually I had learned a lot about purchasing systems. I gained a reputation for flexibility. Once one of the experienced guys had a client who wasn't happy with the system we'd set up, so he came to me. He asked for my advice. I was very flattered. We worked well together because I came with all kinds of ideas about how to manipulate the systems, and he knew the client. We're still close friends.
Interviewer:	That kind of teamwork can be most rewarding. Give me an example of a situation where you found it difficult to work with a team. (flipside)
Candidate:	This situation happened when I worked for Piser, Inc., my last job. There was a team of us charged with working on a specific project. My boss pulled the group together. It was a virtual team with people from all over the world. This group

never gelled. There was a lot of posturing and bickering about the task. We worked for over six months and really never accomplished what we set out to do.

Interviewer: What did you learn from that experience? (probe)

This example illustrates the use of the prominent intentional listening skills. There may have been instances, however, when the interviewer could have chosen a reflection, a reality test, or a summary and perhaps strengthened the interview.

In Chapter 9, we complete the picture with the remaining three intentional listening skills. By knowing all the skills, you have more options open to you. A skillfully placed reality test or reflection might yield even deeper information from this candidate. For example, when the candidate explained his frustration over working with the nonfunctional virtual group, the interviewer could have said, "That sounds like a very frustrating experience." Leaving out that reflection and going directly to the probe keeps the candidate at a distance. Your goal in the strategic interview is to bring the candidate closer to you.

PRACTICE EXERCISE

1. Write a probe response for each of the following candidate statements.
   a. Interviewer: What is the most important aspect of the job you're seeking?
      Candidate: It has to be challenging.

   b. Interviewer: What makes you want to work for Sanders Company?
      Candidate: I want to work for a progressive company.

   c. Interviewer: Describe some of your professional successes.
      Candidate: I was elected spokesperson for the team.

   d. Interviewer: I noticed on your résumé that you held two jobs last year, one for a short time. Tell me what happened in that job.
      Candidate: My boss was real hard to work for. I worked hard but we just couldn't get along. So I got another job.

2. Write a *paraphrase* response for each of the following candidate statements.
   a. Candidate: In my last job I had lots of freedom.

   b. Candidate: I really enjoy working with people rather than sitting in front of a computer all day.

   c. Candidate: My hobbies include reading and skiing. I usually go to Denver once a year for a week-long skiing trip. It's become a family tradition.

    d. Candidate: I traveled a lot in my last job and rarely had time to do anything at home except pack my suitcase. I loved the work and the experiences once I got to wherever I was going.

3. Write a *flipside* response to the following candidate statement.

Interviewer: Tell me about your experiences on the Excel project with the management team.

Candidate: I lead a group of 16 people. We met twice a week for the first six months of the project. Then we cut down to once a week. The experience taught me a lot about how to manage a group, especially one that large and that diverse. I enjoyed the sharing and the breath of experience in the room. Often I'd leave a meeting overwhelmed with how much the people knew in our company. The project was a great success. Afterward we celebrated as a team. It was hard to break up when the project ended.

See Appendix A for sample responses.

NINE

Less Prominent Intentional Listening Skills: Summary, Reality Test, and Reflection

Even though this chapter examines the less prominent intentional listening skills, you must not assume these skills are any less important. In reality, you want to use *all* the intentional listening skills with equal proficiency. Nonetheless, in interviews you will find yourself using the summary, reality test, and reflection less frequently than the probe, paraphrase, and flipside. As such, they play a lesser role in the interview environment. If, however, you find that you are often never using these skills in your interviews, you may want to reevaluate your purpose. These skills do have a purpose, and when that purpose arises, you want to use them. When a candidate clearly expresses feelings, you should not respond with a paraphrase. In this chapter we'll examine some examples of this common interviewing mistake.

The goal of this chapter is to take each of the less prominent intentional listening skills and look at them in depth. As with the prominent intentional listening skills, the less prominent ones have a particular aim. You would not use a summary unless you had a reason to do so—always bearing in mind your ultimate goal: to get the candidate to tell you something he's got locked securely in his hidden area.

THE PURPOSE OF SUMMARIES AND HOW TO ASK THEM

A summary is defined exactly as you might expect: it pulls together what was said in a shorter form. Usually a summary is a series of paraphrases. But it need not be a series of paraphrases; it could be one paraphrase that captures everything a candidate said. Summaries take on many forms but have one commonality: they reduce what was said to a capsule form. Let's look at an example:

Interviewer:	Tell me what made you decide to leave your last job.
Candidate:	I worked for the Amber-Gold Corporation for over 10 years. It was a great experience for me. As it was my first job out of college, I had an opportunity to apply everything I learned about marketing there. We launched some awesome campaigns, and by the time I left, I was heading up many of them. But I had reached the top of the ladder, at least as far as marketing management went. My boss, the vice president for marketing, was not planning on going anywhere, and he was years away from retirement. The only way for me to grow and progress was to move on. I hated leaving, but I knew I had to.
Interviewer:	So it sounds as if you enjoyed the challenges at Amber-Gold and what you learned there, but you could no longer grow in that company—that you basically reached the top there.

The interviewer digested everything the candidate said and said it back to her in a shorter, more condensed form.

If you reread the candidate response, you might see opportunities for some probes; for example, "When you headed campaigns, what did you do?" or "What kinds of things about marketing did you learn while working for Amber-Gold?" Indeed there are several places an interviewer may wish to probe, but first it is a good idea to use a summary, for the following reasons:

- To take a long bit of information and cull it down to your key points. In this example the interviewer is interested in the candidate's ambition.
- If you are team interviewing, to cue your interview partner that you have completed a line of inquiry and are ready for her to take over.
- To give yourself time to think about everything the candidate said. A summary is actually an opportunity to think out loud.
- To break up a series of probes. A paraphrase works well to break up a series of probes, but when the probes are digging into the same subject matter, a summary is a better choice. The following is an example:

Interviewer:	What was your role on the project team?
Candidate:	I represented the marketing division. The team was made up of people from all parts of the company. Our job was to bring to market a new product. We wanted to get it out there in just the right way. There were people on the team from sales, from development, as well as from corporate. Marketing was just one aspect, but in my view the most important part.
Interviewer:	So how did you relate to all these different parts?

Candidate: Actually, it was hard at first. In fact, because I felt marketing had such a vital role, I had trouble listening to ideas put forth by the sales guy. He talked a lot about the people in his district. I couldn't see where that mattered. But after a while I saw his input as a good way to determine how people might accept the product. He had a perfect little focus group there for us.

Interviewer: What about the corporate people—how did they contribute?

Candidate: They had lots to say about history and how products were launched in the past. They also helped us see what we could do within our budget constraints. Their contribution played a key role in the final launch plan we agreed to.

Interviewer: To summarize a bit, it sounds as if even though you found it hard at first, you learned that the others on the team had much to contribute to make the product launch a success. I also get the impression that you recognized their value much more as you continued to work with them.

Candidate: That's a good assessment.

Interviewer: Give me an example of something that happened that helped you change your view of the team.

Notice how this interviewer asked three probes before tossing in a summary to capture the important information from those previous probes and then continued to probe further.

The following are common ways to introduce a summary:

- Let me see if I heard everything you said. . . .
- Perhaps I could summarize what you said . . .
- In summary . . .
- If I heard what you've said correctly, I might summarize by saying . . .

THE PURPOSE OF REALITY TESTS AND HOW TO ASK THEM

One of the most difficult intentional listening skills is the reality test because it requires paying close attention to all cues. If you are not careful, a reality test could sound sarcastic. Reality tests say to a candidate, "We're colleagues who trust one another, so let's be straight with each other. Is this what you really mean to say?" As you can see, the reality test cannot happen until a certain amount of rapport has been established in the interview. With some candidates you might establish rapport very quickly; with others it may take longer, or you may never establish the kind of rapport necessary to employ a reality test.

As defined, a reality test assesses the truth of what's been said. You don't want to say, "Is that really true?" But you do want to say, "Let me see if I'm clear on what you mean." Psychologically you are saying to the candidate, *I respect you enough to be open and honest; I hope you respect me in the same way.* If a candidate says something outrageous and you let it go by, you give the impression that the candidate can tell you anything, and you'll believe him. Reality tests put you and the candidate on an equal footing. Let's look at an example:

Interviewer:	What difficulties would you encounter having to work some nights and weekends?
Candidate:	I would have no difficulties. I can work any time and would love the opportunity to work nights and weekends. In fact, I think it would be nice to be going to work when other people are off because there wouldn't be as much traffic on the roads. I'm sure I'd have to get used to it, but I tend to be a very flexible person and can adjust to most anything. I'm not a person who has ever had a routine.
Interviewer:	Am I clear that you've never had to work night shifts or weekends?
Candidate:	That's right. All my jobs have been strictly eight- to-five kind of jobs, but I'm sure I wouldn't mind the variation in hours. It couldn't be that hard to adjust.
Interviewer:	I respect your willingness to try something new, but I want to be clear on what you're saying. Are you saying you would have no difficulties in adjusting to a schedule where you sleep while others work and you work while others sleep?

In this example, because the candidate had never had the experience of working nights and weekends, it makes the believability of his desire to do so more unlikely. Nonetheless, the interviewer softened the reality test by showing respect for the candidate first. *Most instances of reality testing occur when candidates clearly try to tell you something they think you want to hear rather than the actual truth.* They are not consciously saying something false. They are simply giving you a lighthearted answer that they hope you will ignore. Let's look at another example:

Interviewer:	What are your future educational plans?
Candidate:	Actually, I've not thought about future graduate work. I'm happy to be finished with school and looking forward to starting my career.
Interviewer:	With grades like yours, it's hard for me to believe the faculty hasn't pressured you to go on for your master's degree.
Candidate:	My econ professor did talk to me about pursuing an MBA, and I did think about it a bit, but it's not what I want to do right now. I want to figure out what I enjoy about business

before I make any future educational plans, and I may decide
I've had enough education if I get the right job.

Interviewer: So you have thought about your MBA, but you are not ready
to pursue it right now, correct?

Notice how the reality test enabled the candidate to elaborate on her future
plans. A less skillful interviewer may have let the first response go and never
gotten to the deeper answer.

Purpose of a Reality Test

Reality tests are used in a strategic interview when you hear something you
either doubt or you know isn't completely true. *The purpose is not to trick the
candidate or to embarrass him. The purpose is to show the candidate that you
heard what he said and you want clarity.* Your goal is to simply test the veracity
of the statement by putting it in a different perspective. After a reality test, candidates will often say something like, "Well, when you put it like that . . . ," or
"In that situation, I can see where you'd think. . . ."

Lawyers trick witnesses on the stand with reality testing. Our purpose is not to
trick but to clarify with as much certainty as we can. The candidate in the above
example still has a chance to clarity her statement with something like, "Yes,
I suppose I did give graduate school some thought, but I decided against it."

Common mistakes interviewers make with reality testing include the following:

- Ignoring those things that don't quite jive
- Employing a reality test before rapport has been established
- Using nonverbal cues that suggest sarcasm, such as looking away or
  emphasizing words that suggest disbelief.

Unlike the other intentional listening skills, there is no common way to begin
a reality test. Essentially, you can use a lot of variation to achieve your results.

Table 9.1   Examples of Reality Test Responses

Candidate Response	Follow-Up RealityTest
My ideas are what made our group succeed.	So you're saying you were responsible for the group's success?
I'm sure I won't mind working weekends.	You've said you've never worked weekends but you think you won't mind weekend work?
I've hardly ever had a conflict I couldn't handle.	Am I clear that you're saying you could handle any conflict that might arise?

The two examples we saw earlier show two different kinds of reality tests. The first was an example of a paraphrase with an attitude—probably the most common. The second was a statement, not a question, but with the underlying feel of a reality test.

The examples of reality tests in Table 9.1 show how to use this skill to encourage candidates to be honest with you.

THE PURPOSE OF REFLECTIONS AND HOW TO ASK THEM

Although reflections are not the most difficult intentional listening skill, some interviewers struggle with them. The key is learning how to listen for *feelings*. Our use of reflection in an interview is different from reflective listening as described by Carl Rogers. Rogerian psychologists use reflective listening to do more than reflect feelings. They seek to understand a person's motivation and to offer ideas or suggestions around that understanding. You do not do that in an interview. *You simply want to reflect back feelings in order to create a deeper rapport with the candidate.*

A reflection is defined as a response that mirrors the feelings you hear expressed. As we stated in Chapter 7, often these feelings come through the candidate's nonverbal cues. For example, if a candidate frowns while telling you about a conflict he had with an employee, you might say, "It looks as if that employee caused you some stress." Stress is the feeling you see from the nonverbal cue—frowning. Again, just like with all the intentional listening skills, you end the statement with an elevation of your voice to indicate a question: "It looks as if that employee caused you some stress?"

One of the biggest problems interviewers have with reflection is identifying the feeling they hear. Instead of using a reflection, they use a paraphrase, which is fine except a reflection might bring you closer to the candidate and help you build rapport sooner. Remember our ultimate goal: to get the candidate to tell you something he didn't intend to tell you, to share something from that elusive hidden area, in essence to trust you.

Let's look at an example:

Interviewer: I see you left the armed services after 15 years. How was that for you?

Candidate: I must say it was a tough decision. My dad was in the army, and I grew up thinking I'd be a military man. When I entered the navy after high school, it seemed like the most natural thing in the world for me to do. I learned my trade in the military. I grew up there. But, after 15 years, it was clearly time for me to move on. I was tired of traveling and being away from my family. They didn't want to live on base. So it boiled down to either my family or the military.

Interviewer: Gosh, that sounds like a very hard choice. It must have been very soul searching for you.

How did this interviewer reflect feelings? Is "soul-searching" a feeling? Even though this interviewer did a nice job with her paraphrase, she did not reflect the candidate's feelings because soul-searching is not a feeling. Here are some examples that illustrate a reflection in this instance.

- You sound very sad to have left the military.
- I can't imagine having to make that kind of decision. It must have caused you a lot of stress.
- I hear some disappointment in your decision to leave the military.
- A soul-searching decision like that can cause a lot of anxiety. How did you deal with that anxiety?

Notice the different ways the interviewer might express a reflection and the depth of feeling the interviewer might choose. Sadness and stress are feelings, but not deep emotional feelings. Anxiety is a bit deeper. Depending on the nonverbal cues you get from the candidate, you choose the depth of feeling you wish to reflect back. For example instead of saying, "You sound angry about leaving the military," (a volatile feeling), you might say, "You sound frustrated about leaving the military" (a less volatile feeling).

The Purpose of a Reflection

As we've said, reflections pave the way toward building trust and rapport. The Johari window taught you about the importance of bringing candidates closer to you in order to build trust. Reflections are ways to do that, but just like with the reality test, you wouldn't want to reflect—particularly if you choose to reflect a more volatile feeling, like anger or rage—early in the interview. People feel violated if you reflect too soon. Furthermore, just like with all the intentional listening skills, you don't want to reflect too much. Imagine a situation like this:

Interviewer: How was it working with a virtual team that you could never see face-to-face?

Candidate: At first I was bothered by it and didn't think we'd ever get past the bickering. People didn't seem to care anything about people's feelings. They argued over every little detail, even when we tried to plan our next meeting.

Interviewer: That must have been very frustrating for you as team leader.

Candidate: It sure was. I tried to keep people on task and let them know what we had to do when, but every time we connected,

	people rehashed the same old stuff, over and over. Before long people began missing meetings. I know they were as ready as I was to chuck it all.
Interviewer:	I'm sure that made you mad.
Candidate:	I wasn't exactly mad, but I did dread the meetings. I had no choice, though; I had to go.
Interviewer:	That must have really stressed you out.

Enough already! The first reflection was a nice one, but by the second and third, the candidate started shutting down. As this example illustrates, you want to use reflection, but sparingly.

The following are some typical ways to initiate a reflection, remembering the understood question mark at the end of the sentence.

- It sounds as if . . .
- If I'm hearing you correctly, you felt . . .
- You sound . . .
- What I'm hearing is that you felt . . .
- Are you saying you felt . . .

Just like with the other intentional listening skills, it is important that you vary your approaches to reflections. If you say, "So you're feeling . . ." every time, your reflections begin to sound trite. Also, with reflection, even more so than with the other intentional listening skills, you must really listen. You cannot tune out and then reflect. When you say to someone you hear a feeling, you need to get as close as possible to that feeling. If you say you hear stress and the person just communicated pride—oops. You've definitely lost that candidate's trust.

The examples of reflections in Table 9.2 show how to use a reflection to gain a candidate's trust.

Table 9.2 Examples of Reflection Responses

Candidate Response	Follow-Up Reflections
My boss tends to micromanage my work.	To have someone looking over your shoulder must be frustrating.
I've been on the Dean's List every semester since I've been in school.	You must be really proud of that accomplishment.
I hate it when people don't believe I can do a task and they treat me like a two-year-old.	Sounds as if you get really annoyed when people underestimate your abilities.

INTERVIEW EXAMPLE USING ALL SIX INTENTIONAL LISTENING SKILLS

Interviewer: Good morning, Miss Seymour. Thank you for coming today. I'm Janice Welch, a lead interviewer for our company. I see you majored in history at Columbia University. I did, too.

Seymour: You majored in history, too? That's amazing.

Interviewer: Is Dr. Russell still dean?

Seymour: He is, and I was lucky enough to have him for a course on the Civil War.

Interviewer: So did I! I didn't know he still taught. When I went to school, he wasn't dean, but I really enjoyed his class. I was delighted when he was appointed.

Seymour: I loved all my classes, including that one. Going to school was one of the best experiences in my life.

Interviewer: Yes, too bad we don't usually realize that while we're in school. I had an unusual college experience. I worked full time and went to school part time. So I didn't benefit from a true college experience.

Seymour: I've had to work, too, but only part time. School is my full-time work.

Interviewer: You say school was a great experience. What made that experience so good?

Comment: At this point the interviewer has moved out of the icebreaker and directly into the interview. Notice how the icebreaker conversation flowed naturally. The interviewer shared lots of information about herself in this segment.

Seymour: Mainly the classes. The entire history curriculum was such fun. There wasn't a course I didn't learn something in. You can really learn about people by studying history.

Interviewer: Tell me how history has helped you learn about people.

Comment: Here the interviewer chose to use a probe in order to learn more about the candidate's vague comment about people. Clearly, working with people is one of her target competencies.

Seymour: Gosh, you see all kinds of people in history. And sometimes they do foolish things, just like all of us. My summer job with Holy Methodist helped me use what I've learned about people in a practical way.

Interviewer: I'm particularly interested in that position you had with the church. Tell me more about that.

Seymour:	That was a great experience, even as a summer job. I came to work all excited and ready to change the world.
Interviewer:	How did that position live up to your expectations?
Seymour:	My boss was super. He gave me all kinds of leeway. I went in as the campaign manager for the capital funds drive for the church's building project. I had never done anything like that before, but I researched what other churches had done and discovered lots of information. I designed my own campaign and involved many volunteers. There was so much energy and enthusiasm. My boss, the minister, helped me when necessary, but mostly he left me alone.
Interviewer:	So, without any experience in capital funds drives, you spearheaded one single-handedly?

Comment: Wow! The interview tossed in a reality test very soon. How was she able to risk doing that? She worked so hard in the initial part of the interview creating trust. Furthermore, this reality test sounds teasing rather than threatening. Let's see how the candidate took it.

Seymour:	(Laughs) Not exactly like a superwoman. I had lots of help and support. The Methodist Church has consultants to help with these things and lots of how-to literature. I made use of everything I could. Also, the volunteers were great. We had professional people in our church whose jobs entailed development and fundraising. One man, in particular, helped me develop my plan. He took me through it step by step. I learned more from him than any of my college professors.
Interviewer:	So what you are saying then is you made use of all the information available to you and all the people you could to design the capital funds drive?

Comment: Here the interviewer used a summary paraphrase to positively present what the candidate did to organize the capital funds drive. The purpose was to strengthen the candidate's rapport (in case the reality test threatened it) and to take a lot of information and boil it down to the key target competencies.

Seymour:	Absolutely. I've learned if you pretend to be an expert, people will watch you fail. But if you go in with an open mind, willing to listen to others, they'll join in and help. No campaign will succeed unless the organization buys into it.
Interviewer:	You sound pretty confident in what you've learned in your work experience, even though that experience has been limited.

Comment: The interviewer reflected the feeling of confidence back to the candidate. Again, rapport is strong enough for the interviewer to choose a reflection, but she selected a nonvolatile feeling.

Seymour: Perhaps I am confident about some things. I have learned a lot, but I'm sure there's a lot more to learn.

Interviewer: You say you learned that people must buy into a campaign plan for it to work. How did you manage to get people on board?

Comment: The interviewer probed here to piggy-back what the candidate said previously and to dig deeper into her target competencies (people management and leadership).

Seymour: I set up committees. At the church they consisted of volunteers. Each committee had a task, and all were linked.

Interviewer: What did some of these committees do?

Seymour: I had a committee that identified and called donors; another committee was in charge of the publicity and communication; another worked on the budget.

Interviewer: So you had committees working on all the major campaign functions.

Comment: The interviewer broke up her probes with a paraphrase for two reasons: (1) to give the candidate a break from too many questions and (2) to clarify what the candidate said.

Seymour: I did. I oversaw everything, but there was an active committee chair. We also had a steering committee. Members of that committee sat on all the other committees to maintain consistency.

Interviewer: I've worked with volunteer committees before. It can be a very useful way to get work done, but it can also be frustrating. What frustrations did you encounter?

Comment: This is an example of a flipside. The interviewer has only heard positive things about this candidate's experience with committees. It's time to hear what might not be so positive. Notice how the interviewer threw in her own knowledge of committees. She continues to build rapport by sprinkling in bits about herself as she goes.

Seymour: I won't say I didn't pull my hair out. Working with volunteers is quite a challenge. As you said, it can be useful and rewarding. But there are inherent problems. Some volunteers don't really get involved. They stay on the outside. They agree

	to do things and then never come through. But what's equally difficult are the volunteers who get too involved and want to take over. They shut others out. I've had experiences with both.
Interviewer:	Give me an example of how you handled a situation where a volunteer overstepped the boundaries.

Comment: This is a good example of a behavior-based probe.

Seymour:	There have been several situations. The most obvious happened not long after I began working at the church. One man had spent two years surveying the church community about the possibility of a new building project. He was a volunteer, but he had spent hours on this issue. He was a great person, really committed to the church and the plan, but he wanted it done his way. He felt we needed to immediately solicit donors. He didn't want to spend any more time talking about stuff. He had collected a lot of information, but it was from a small segment of the population. I thought we needed a broader base. You see, being a history major, I respect what people have done in the past. This church had a lot of history of failed campaigns for just that reason. Anyway, convincing this man to do more research wasn't easy.
Interviewer:	How did you manage to convince him?

Comment: In this instance the interviewer demonstrates how to construct a behavior-based probe by paraphrasing the words the candidate said.

Seymour:	I'm not sure how it happened, but I think my naïveté helped. Others told me later that he had turned off lots of people with his demanding, know-it-all personality. Because everything was new to me, I solicited his help. I innocently asked him questions he couldn't answer. When he realized I wasn't going to plunge ahead without more work and when he couldn't answer the questions I posed, he caved. It was interesting. At first, he told me what to do; by the time I left the church, we worked easily together.
Interviewer:	Working with someone like that can zap all your energy. How did you manage not to lose your enthusiasm?
Seymour:	I believe I did lose a little at first. I became disillusioned and frustrated. Rather than get on with a project I was really excited about, I spent hours smoothing out the feathers this man ruffled. He left a lot of broken people in his wake. But after a bit, people began to trust me. They wanted to see the project succeed. That helped.

Interviewer: So when people began to trust you, what happened to you?
Seymour: I started getting excited again. We basically diluted the power of this man. I won't say it was easy. I was consumed in it the first month I was at the church. But after that, he sort of disappeared. He remained active, but in the background.
Interviewer: Dealing with this man sounded like a frustrating experience. I'm not sure I'd have had the patience to keep going.

Comment: After several probes and paraphrases, the interviewer threw in a reflection. She did it by sharing how she might respond to this situation in order to continue to build trust and rapport with the candidate.

Seymour: I did lose patience. There's no question about that. But my experience with him also threatened to break down my confidence. Looking back now, I see how much that experience taught me. I learned that we can't let others overstep boundaries, even when they're not volunteers. I learned that if we don't have clear boundaries, others will overstep. I finally managed to give this man clear boundaries. He seemed to respect that. Others did, too.
Interviewer: If I'm hearing you, boundaries sound as if they're very important in your human interactions. How do you deal with situations when the boundaries aren't clear because the organization doesn't want boundaries?

Comment: Here we have a summary paraphrase that leads into the next area to probe. This is the best use of summary. It takes everything that has been said and reduces it down to the major point, in this case boundaries.

Seymour: If you're talking about creative situations, I have some trouble there. I don't consider myself a real creative person. I also don't see myself as a risk taker. I like to work within boundaries, and I can excel in that environment. A real loose organization without boundaries drives me nuts.

Comment: Finally we reach a place where the candidate is revealing things about herself she did not intend to say when she walked in the door. She is honestly assessing her weaknesses. What the candidate tells the interviewer will help her determine if this candidate is a fit for her job. If the job is more free flowing and without clear boundaries, this candidate may not be a good fit. This interviewer accomplished what she set out to do: she built rapport and strategically used each of the intentional listening skills order to get the candidate to divulge a piece of information from her hidden area.

In this chapter you've had a chance to explore the less prominent intentional listening skills. During the interview with Seymour you discovered how using all the intentional listening skills, the prominent and the less prominent, enabled the interviewer to chip away at the superficial. A less skillful interviewer might not have learned as much about Seymour and could have likely hired her for a job where she was not suited. As this chapter demonstrated, when you conduct a strategic interview with the POINT process, you are in a better position to hire smart and keep 'em.

PRACTICE EXERCISE

1. Write a *summary* response for the following candidate statement.
   Interviewer: Looking over your career, tell me what prompted you to move from sales to training.
   Candidate: I suppose it was a number of things rather than just one event. I had worked in direct sales from the time I sold magazines in high school. It seemed no matter what career options I pursued, I fell into sales. I suppose that meant I was good at it. Anyway, after working for six years with Billings Company, selling the product, traveling from pillar to post, I became restless. I wanted to challenge myself to do something else. I began teaching people how to better use the product. I was interested in selling it, but I became more interested in product retention by teaching others how to better use it. This was a new idea at the time and created lots of interest among the management team. One thing led to another, and before long I was teaching the sales force about product retention and creating new ideas for usage.

2. Write a *reality test* response for each of the following candidate statements.
   a. Candidate: Even though I've never worked on teams, I love people, and a job that enables me to interact with others is exactly what I am looking for.
   b. Candidate: When it comes to hard work, I'm the one. I'm the kind of person who never gets tired. I could work 80 hours a week and never even feel it.

3. Write a *reflection* response for each of the following candidate statements.
   a. Candidate: I really don't like doing the same thing over and over again.
   b. Candidate: Working the night shift is too much work.
   c. Candidate: Between my scholarship and my part-time job, I managed to pay for my entire college education.
   d. Candidate: When I decided to leave my last job, my supervisor told me I could come back anytime. I really couldn't believe she felt that way.

See Appendix A for sample responses.

TEN

Testing the Effectiveness of the Interview: Deciding Whom to Hire

Because the interview lies at the heart of any hiring decision, we placed the interview at the center of the action. We looked at the importance of conducting behavior-based interviews that focus on past behavior. We studied how to keep interviews open by creating and building trust in the interview environment, and we explored the listening skills necessary to get at the truth during an employment interview. You learned that a quality strategic interview, whether as a team or solo, focuses on the candidate and uses advanced listening skills to learn more than surface information. With all that under your belt, you are clearly in a much better position to hire smart than you were before you started.

Adler says, "While the performance-based interview should represent the heart of the hiring decision, it needs to be supplemented with other tools."[1] He goes on to say that if you conduct a competent and careful interview, you'll be about 75 percent accurate.[2]

Given that you want to be at least 80 percent accurate to hire smart and keep em', there are two important points you still must consider. First, did you conduct a competent and careful interview? And second, what other tools might help you raise the odds?

In this chapter we will look at the T in the POINT process—tests. *The T tests everything you've done and puts those actions under the microscope to determine if you indeed accomplished your goals.* To hire smart and keep em,' you want to apply the T before you make a final decision.

WHAT TESTS ARE APPROPRIATE IN THE INTERVIEW ENVIRONMENT

The literature and best practices for interviews show widespread disagreement about tests. Some people believe testing to be the magical tool for smart interviewing. Others recognize that testing cannot provide all the answers. For example, Erling wrote, "Used correctly, psychological assessments can offer great value in the hiring process,"[3] while Adler said, "Personality-related tests are pretty useless."[4] Both, however, went on to add a caveat: Erling said that the bottom line is that companies who depend too much on psychological tests are not as successful with their hiring decisions. Adler conceded that the most appropriate tests are those that measure job-related skills. Given these discrepancies in thinking, what are managers to do?

Some companies add testing to their hiring mix. In other words, they conduct solid strategic interviews, check references, and administer tests before making a decision. That's a fine solution, but what do you do in a situation like this: You conduct a strategic interview with a candidate whom you wish to hire. Recalling what Adler said, namely that your decision is likely to be 75 percent accurate (if you conducted a competent and careful interview), you should feel fairly confident about your decision. Your company gives the candidate a psychological test, and she fails to meet the testing standards. What do you do? Start all over? Before you answer these questions, you must determine two things:

1. How effective were the strategic interviews? Later in this chapter we will look at ways for you to evaluate the strategic interview. Meantime, you must recognize that sometimes perceptions are so strong they lead you astray. Mornell talked about several instances in which people "fell in love" with the candidate[5] and no matter what they heard in the interview or what others thought, they wanted to hire. He likened the phenomenon to a courtship and marriage. When you fall in love with someone, you often do not see the flaws and blemishes. If you've ever had this happen, you know how dangerous it can be. Given the power of perception, you cannot assume because you feel a candidate is a good fit that you conducted a solid strategic interview. That assumption must be tested.

2. What do the tests measure? Tests that measure personality do just that. The Myers-Briggs Type Indicator®, the DISC,[*] Personality Inventory® or the plethora of similar instruments on the market tell you about personality style. They do not tell you if the person is a serial killer or a compulsive liar. These instruments reveal personality traits. For example, they might show that a person's behavior style is more intuitive or less analytical than another person's. If you are filling a job that requires strong analytical skills, these tests can help you determine a tendency in that direction. If you are filling a job that requires an outgoing personality that flourishes when working with people, these tests can help you determine those preferences. I would argue that a

---

*DISC stands for Dominance, Influence, Steadiness, and Compliance. Developed by John Geier based on the 1928 work of William Merton. www.discprofile.com

good strategic interview based on past performance can also help you make these determinations with equal accuracy.

Clearly, then, a discrepancy between a strategic interview and test results registers a red flag. You must go back to your interviews and examine them with an eye for perception biases, and you must examine your tests to determine what they are telling you.

PERSONALITY TESTING

As we stated, personality tests sometimes tell you what you need to know and sometimes do not. *Companies that rely too much on these tests often make drastic hiring mistakes.* Nonetheless the tests do have some value if used carefully. Let's look at what they do and don't tell you.

- One of the biggest values of personality testing is consistency. When making judgments about people, it is very hard not to bring in your personal feelings (perceptions). Personality tests do not have personal feelings. They ask the same questions of everyone without bias.
- One of the biggest problems with personality tests is that the results come from the individual taker's perception of behavior. Bear in mind the person taking the test interprets the question according to what that person believes to be true. In other words, if he believes he's analytical, he will respond accordingly whether or not he really is. This phenomenon represents a fatal flaw in personality testing.

We're back to square one. What does the manager do?

My recommendation: do not use personality testing for hiring decisions. My reason for this recommendation is too many people believe the results and blindly follow those results. If the results indicate not to hire, the costs to the company are minimal. Unfortunately, when the results indicate to hire, the costs are huge. Candidates know how to respond to these tests. If the candidate knows you are looking for a person with strong leadership abilities, she will answer the questions accordingly. Going back to what you know about strategic interviewing, the best predictor of a person's behavior is not what she scores on a test but what she has done in the past. You might also note that some law enforcement agencies use lie-detector tests in combination with other testing to screen candidates. But even lie-detector tests have flaws. Some people—particularly the people those agencies are trying to eliminate—know how to fool the lie detector. The human being is smarter than any test yet devised!

Although I recommend your company avoid personality testing for hiring decisions, I realize some companies will do so anyway. If your company does decide to use personality tests, I suggest you use them judiciously. In other words, if there is a great discrepancy in the test and what you learned in your strategic interviews, do not simply believe the test. Put both assumptions under scrutiny with equal intensity.

If only there was a miracle test that could tell you whether or not to hire someone! If such an instrument existed, we could put away our interview gear and simply administer tests. Unfortunately, no such test exists, and I doubt very seriously that one ever will. Tests are simply another piece of information in the interview arsenal. They provide another way to look at particular skills. They do not answer the basic question: can this candidate do the job?

HOW TO TEST WHETHER A CANDIDATE FITS YOUR JOB

Based on everything you've seen on the résumé and the responses you've heard in the interview, the basic question is whether this candidate can do the job. This is the fundamental decision managers struggle to make. You've seen the pitfalls of psychological testing. What about the pitfalls inherent with the interview?

What the Interview Can and Cannot Tell You

Interviews tell you less than you may realize. One common mistake among managers is to believe interviews reveal more than they actually do. As you examine the effectiveness of your interview, you must look at it realistically.

In my first book on interviewing,[6] I listed the following factors and asked which of these candidate attributes can you *easily* determine during the interview:

1. Philosophy and objectives
2. Reason for choosing your organization
3. General career aspirations
4. Background
5. Interests and hobbies
6. Attitude
7. Enthusiasm
8. Willingness to accept criticism
9. Loyalty
10. Ability to solve problems
11. Job performance
12. Missing information
13. Physical appearance

14. Ability to appraise strengths and weaknesses
15. Intelligence
16. Poise under pressure

If you selected "reason for choosing your organization" (2), "general career aspirations" (3), "interests and hobbies" (5), "missing information" (12), "physical appearance" (13), "ability to appraise strengths and weaknesses" (14), and "poise under pressure" (16), you are correct. You cannot ascertain the remaining items *easily* in an interview. You might think the candidate is intelligent, but how can an interview accurately tell you that? You might *sense* a candidate is loyal, but how can an interview accurately tell you that? Erling wrote: "The biggest blind spot hiring managers have in our recruiting experience is that they believe that their intuition will guide them to a correct hire."[7] As managers who want to hire smart, you must not depend solely on your intuition. Strategic interviewing enables you to get past that murky water. If loyalty is a target competency, you must determine what loyalty means and create a strong strategic line of questioning that uncovers information about loyalty.

Value of Reference Checking

Besides the interview, the second most important tool you have to help you make your decision is reference checking. Learning how the person performed on her last job or her previous several jobs is a vital piece of information. Unfortunately, references are harder and harder to get. In *Strategic Interviewing* I wrote, "Because reference information has become evasive at best, the interview ends up being our most valuable resource for determining job performance."[8] Previous employers do not want to share negative information about others because of the fear of litigation. Even college professors who are asked to write letters for their students write vague letters that tell you little about a person's performance. One professor told me, "I didn't want to ruin his chance to get a job." Most companies have a strict policy that states they do not give references. They merely indicate the person's dates of employment, nothing more.

Does this mean you do not check references? Absolutely not! References may not give you much information, but they do give you some. If you are facing a candidate who broke the law, you will discover that information if you do your due diligence. Imagine how embarrassed you'd be if you hired someone and then found out she had committed a felony. You must learn the obvious, and you can do that from online sources and basic reference checking. Learning the not-so-obvious is another story altogether.

Where does this leave managers? You see that testing may or may not give you the information you need to make a hiring decision. Interviews may or may not give you what you need. References provide a vague account about a person's past behavior, and you cannot rely on your intuition. Do you just throw your hands up in frustration?

Tips to Help You Make an Educated Decision

- Don't simply rely on evaluating the candidate. Evaluate the interview and the process. Weigh those factors against what you learned in the strategic interviews.

- Use behavior testing to evaluate skills. That means creating tests that do not measure personality but do measure a person's ability to perform some particular task. These tests need to be behavior specific and not speculative. In other words, do not structure tests with language like, "If you had this kind of situation, what would you do?" This language does not assess past performance. Create tests or opportunities for people to demonstrate skills. For example, many organizations require candidates to give a brief presentation as part of the interviewing process.

- Establish informal relationships with people in your industry. Go to professional organization meetings and join groups in social networks that relate to your work. People are more likely to talk to someone they know, off the record. When that colleague comes to you with a similar request, be sure to return the favor. If you are not comfortable with ever giving references, then do not ask others to do so.

- Use a combination of tools. Don't rely on one source for your decision. Test skills, conduct a variety of strategic interviews, and get references.

- Combine solo interviews with team interviews to cut down on the possibility of perception bias.

Whatever your tools for evaluation, remember you cannot hire someone with absolute, 100 percent accuracy. At some point you must stop and make a decision. Sure, you are taking a risk, but the point is to minimize your risk as much as possible, not eliminate it. The only way to know if someone can do the job with 100 percent accuracy is for him to do the job. The interview and the interview process enable you to make a decision with 80 percent accuracy and thereby increase your odds of hiring smart and keeping 'em.

INTERVIEW EFFECTIVENESS ASSESSMENT

Let's examine an interview and by using the Interview Effectiveness Assessment—Questions to help you rate how effective the strategic interview is (See sidebar).

INTERVIEW EFFECTIVENESS ASSESSMENT

1. What was the interviewer's plan?
2. How much time did the interviewer talk versus listen?
3. What icebreaker did the interviewer use?
4. How did the icebreaker help the candidate open up?
5. When did the interviewer probe with open questions?
6. What strategic reasons did the interviewer have for asking closed questions?
7. Cite examples when the interviewer used other intentional listening skills (paraphrase, reflection, summary, reality test, flipside).
8. How often did the interviewer use behavior-based questions versus future-based questions?
9. How often did the interviewer react to what the candidate said to formulate his or her next question, or how often did the interviewer ask something unrelated to what the candidate said?
10. How did the interviewer react to the candidate's nonverbal cues?
11. In what instances did the interviewer open or self-disclose during the interview?
12. In what instances did the interviewer share information about the job?
13. What could this interviewer do to improve?
14. If you had to grade this interviewer, what grade would you give (A, B, C, D, or F)?

Interviewer: Thank you for coming in today to talk to us about the medical transcription position we have open. My name is Lois Webster, and I'm the director of medical records. May I call you Dale?

Candidate: Yes, please do.

Interviewer: I noticed on your résumé that you play bridge and have been in several competitions. I'm impressed. I recently learned how to play. It's a struggle for me.

Candidate: You've got to stick with it. I learned how to play about five years ago and really got into it. For me, it's a challenge keeping up with the various conventions.

Interviewer: Wow, Dale! You're already miles ahead of me. I'm not sure what a convention is.

Candidate: Players use certain conventions to talk across the table. For example, Goren is one of the most common. But there are

Candidate: many. I like to learn the different ones and practice with them. That helps me keep my skills sharpened.

Interviewer: It sounds as if you're someone who likes to learn new things and stay challenged. How do you keep your skills sharpened with medical transcription?

Candidate: You're right. I do love to learn new things. I think that helps me keep my mind alert as I get older. As for medical transcription, my gosh, there is so much going on and so much to learn. I began with the basic medical terminology, but now I've moved into the specialties. I just learned psychiatric transcription, which is a whole new realm of learning. I do love the opportunity to learn new things and feel personally successful when I grasp something that was hard.

Interviewer: What were some of the biggest challenges you've faced with this kind of learning?

Candidate: For me it was getting comfortable with the technology. It keeps changing. I tend to learn the medical terms quickly, and my hearing is quite good. When a doctor mumbles, I can usually figure out what he means, but sometimes the technology doesn't behave.

Interviewer: I'm like that, too, Dale, I find technology a real pain. As soon as I learn one thing, it either goes away or changes completely. Give me an example of when you had a problem with the technology.

Candidate: When I worked for the regional hospital, we used Norcel dictating equipment. It used to go out as much as it worked. I'd be working along and suddenly everything would go dead. The Norcel reps told us it was because we had too few lines for the volume of work, but I suspected there was a quirk in the system. After I lost a long dictation, I began investigating on my own. I found a system from a competitor that promised never to drop. I told my boss about it. It wasn't an easy sell to the administration, but they finally made the switch.

Interviewer: It sounds as if you were really proud to be part of that change.

Candidate: (Smiles and looks away) Yes, I guess I was. But I didn't get any credit for it.

Interviewer: Is that right? So what happened?

Candidate: Well, that was one of the reasons I left that job. My boss took all the credit. We managed to increase our productivity significantly after the equipment change. He was later promoted and given the highest commendation in the department. He never once mentioned my part in it.

Interviewer: That must have been very distressing.

Candidate: (Sighs and nods) I knew I couldn't keep working there. I found the job with Medical Information Services right after. I've been there ever since.

Interviewer: Going back to that experience with the hospital, what did you learn?

Candidate: (Laughs) If you mean never to trust my boss? Seriously, I learned that people don't always do what's right. Most of the time they do what is best for them.

Interviewer: How have you applied that learning in your current job?

Candidate: Actually, I don't let things bug me. I do my job and try to stay out of the way of the office politics. There's usually a lot of goings on in a transcription environment. I like to keep out of all that.

Interviewer: What do you mean by "goings on"?

Candidate: I think when people are glued to equipment all day and typing as hard as they can, they tend to look for opportunities to talk. There's a lot of gossip. I have trouble with people talking about other people and prefer to stay out of that.

Interviewer: Yes, that is a typical problem in many offices. How have you kept away and not allowed yourself to be drawn in?

Candidate: Mostly I mind my own business and do my work. I don't socialize with the others.

Interviewer: You strike me as a very personable person. I can't imagine you not wanting to go to lunch with your office mates every once in a while.

Candidate: (Uncrosses and recrosses legs) Once in a while I might, but I don't get consumed by the office drama. Some people go out together every day or evening. I will occasionally join them for lunch, but I'm not a regular.

Interviewer: So, let me see if I'm clear. After you got burned by your boss at the hospital, you became more reserved in your relations with colleagues?

Candidate: Yes, I'm sorry it happened, but it's enabled me to be a better employee. I am more interested in doing a quality job than being liked by everyone in the office.

Interviewer: Not being drawn into the office gossip sounds as if it makes you sort of a loner. How has this strategy affected you as a team player?

Candidate: We don't have much teamwork in our office. I enjoy working with others and have done so in the past. But most of the time, I find myself working by myself. When I play bridge I rely a lot on my partner and have learned that we make a good team. I'd like to have that same experience at work.

Interviewer: I take it you miss the feeling of teamwork?

Candidate: One of the reasons I was drawn to your job description is that you said you ran an office that is atypical of most medical transcription offices in that you encourage teamwork. That intrigued me.

Interviewer: Yes, we do a number of projects with partners. I have found that some people handle certain parts of the job better than others, and I like to build on everyone's strengths. When you say you were intrigued by this concept, what intrigued you?

Using the interviewer effectiveness assessment, let's examine this interview, knowing the interviewer is not finished.

What was the interviewer's plan? Can you discern the strategy? This interviewer was striving to uncover what target competencies? My guess is she was looking to determine the candidate's willingness to learn new things and her flexibility. She spent a lot of time probing her about her learning style. As the interview progressed, Lois moved into questions related to interpersonal relations. She seemed to be looking to determine if this candidate might fit with the personality mix she currently has in her office. Clearly the interviewer had a plan.

How much time did the interviewer talk versus listen? The candidate talked at least twice as much as the interviewer. Clearly Lois did not dominate the interview with talk. The interviewer gave the candidate plenty of opportunities to talk.

What icebreaker did the interviewer use? At the outset of the interview, she asked her about her bridge experience, sharing something about herself and her experiences with bridge as well. She didn't spend a lot of time in the icebreaker, but she did give the candidate something easy to talk about in the first few moments of the interview.

How did the icebreaker help the candidate to open up? The icebreaker gave this candidate an opportunity to talk about something comfortable. It enabled her to begin to open up, but she had not completely opened by the end of the icebreaker conversation.

When did the interviewer probe with open questions? Each time Lois probed, she used open questions. For example, the first question she asked was, "How do you keep your skills sharpened with medical transcription?" This question led the interview out of the icebreaker.

What strategic reasons did the interviewer have for asking closed questions? The instances in which Lois asked closed questions were for clarification or to incorporate the other intentional listening skills. Lois never asked a closed question in order to probe.

Cite examples of when the interviewer used other intentional listening skills (paraphrase, reflect, summary, reality test, flipside).

- Paraphrase: "It sounds as though you're someone who likes to learn new things and stay challenged." "Not being drawn into the office gossip sounds as if it makes you sort of a loner." "I take it you miss the feeling of team work."
- Reflect: "It sounds as if you were really proud to be part of that change." "That must have been very distressing."
- Summary: "So, let me see if I'm clear. After you got burned . . ."
- Reality test: "You strike me as a very personable person. I can't imagine you not wanting to go to lunch with your office mates every once in a while."
- Flipside: "What were some of the biggest challenges you've faced with this kind of learning?"

How often did the interviewer use behavior-based questions versus future-based questions? Early in the interview, at the icebreaker, Lois did not use probes. She simply reacted to what the candidate said. She used behavior-based probes later in the interview: "How have you taken the learning into your current job?" "How have you kept away and not allowed yourself to be drawn in?" and "Give me an example of when you had a problem with the technology." Lois never used future-based questions.

How often did the interviewer react to what the candidate said to formulate her next question, or how often did the interviewer ask something unrelated to what the candidate said? In every instance except one, Lois reacted to what the candidate said, using one of the intentional listening skills and piggy-backing what the candidate said. The one instance where she didn't react was when she said, "Is that right? So what happened?" This was not a clear piggy-back. The interviewer asked what happened instead of reacting when the candidate said, "But I didn't get any credit for it." An example of more appropriate response might be, "Not getting credit must have really upset you."

How did the interviewer react to the candidate's nonverbal cues? Since we are examining this interview from a written page, we only saw a couple of nonverbal cues. When the candidate smiled and looked away, Lois noticed something was going on, but she didn't give a good response. She should have reflected or paraphrased here. Later the candidate laughed—we would suspect nervous laughter—and again the interviewer did not pick up on the nonverbal cue. She went right on with her probes.

In what instances did the interviewer open or self-disclose during the interview? At the outset, the interviewer self-disclosed when she said, "I recently learned how to play," and later, "You're already ahead of me. I'm not sure what a convention is." These two comments told the candidate that the interviewer was not going to pretend to know more than the candidate and that she had a healthy respect for the candidate's knowledge. Lois was beginning to chip away at the Johari window Further along in the interview,

Lois continued to share when she said, "I'm like that, too, Dale. I find technology a pain. As soon as you learn one thing, it either goes away or changes completely."

In what instances did the interviewer share information about the job? At the end of the interview, Lois shared a little information about the job when she said, "We do a number of projects with partners. I have found that some people handle certain parts of the job better than others ..."

What could this interviewer do to improve? Clearly this interviewer did a good job using the intentional listening skills. She could have improved by reducing her probes, particularly in the touchy area about the candidate's disappointment with her boss. But the interviewer accomplished what she set out to do: she got the candidate to share something from her hidden area. This candidate probably did not come into this interview planning to tell the interviewer about why she left the hospital. The interviewer might also improve by sharing more information about the job.

If you had to grade this interviewer, what grade would you give (A, B, C, D, or F)? I would give her a B+. I didn't give her an A because I had the feeling the candidate was still holding back. Lois started to develop trust, but she had not gotten there. Had she shared a bit more about herself or shown more compassion with the candidate when she shared her distress over her boss's betrayal, I would increase her grade.

Using the interviewer's effectiveness questions will help you test your interviewing skills. If you asked mostly closed questions when you wanted to probe, for example, and the candidate didn't share a lot of information, you might be at fault, not the candidate. If you did not open with an effective icebreaker and forgot to sprinkle information about yourself and the job into the interview, you could expect your candidate to remain tight-lipped. Determining the effectiveness of the interview will also help you measure your perceptions. If you did not follow your plan, you may have been zapped by a perception.

In addition to testing yourself as an interviewer and how effective you are in the interview environment, you must also test the process—what happens to the candidate from the initial contact to the final interview. If the process breaks down, you can lose your best candidates.

WAYS TO EVALUATE THE RECRUITING PROCESS

The best interviewing skills in the world will fail and hiring mistakes will happen if the process fails.

A process that works contains the following:

• Screen candidates thoroughly before inviting them to interview at your facility (see Chapter 2).

- Develop a team approach to the planning phases of the POINT process. A group of managers comprising the interviewing team determines the qualifications needed and screens the résumés. Don't leave all decisions up to the human resource professionals or solo interviewers.

- Give the candidates a general schedule when they visit your site. *Make sure interviewers have a detailed schedule and stay on time.*

- Prior to initiating interviews, the team discusses the attributes and decides who will focus on what areas. The team determines whether or not to conduct team interviews and pairs themselves accordingly.

- Do not plan interviews around meals. Candidates cannot respond and eat at the same time; interviewers cannot apply the POINT process and eat, too.

- Give the candidate a through tour of your facility.

- After one interviewer finishes with a candidate, that interviewer tags the next interviewer. This means she tells the next interviewer what she covered and what she omitted. *She doesn't share her feelings about the candidate's suitability, either verbally or nonverbally.*

- When the interviewers complete all the interviews, they meet as a team to select the best-suited person. They examine the pros and cons for selecting one person over another. They should not discuss candidates until this final meeting.

In Chapter 4 we discussed the dangers of groupthink. Groupthink can be as deadly to an interview process as perceptions are to a single interview. Let's examine a meeting in progress. As you study this meeting, think about what the team manager did to avoid groupthink.

This meeting occurred after a full day of interviews. Sam, Pete, Lonny, and Jane sit down to discuss their interviews with the first of their three candidates, Marsha Martinson. Pete presides.

Pete: Have each of you individually given your numeric score of Marsha, from 1 to 5, with 1 being "hire immediately"? (All nod or murmur "yes.")

Lonny: I gave Marsha a 2. When I explored her creative skills, I was impressed. She worked as a graduate lab assistant at Oxford. There she performed sum-frequency and laser vibrational spectroscopy. But what really impressed me was her versatility. She sold Lebanese specialty foods at an Oxford deli and fine antiques at an antique store in Oxford to earn extra money. She's also a classical violinist, and she flies airplanes!

Jane: Yeah, I liked Marsha as well. I gave her a 2 because she seemed really well versed in physical chemistry. Of course, she's getting her doctorate from Oxford University and she has a masters in chem from the University of Chicago. Clearly, she's got the technical skills we're looking for. When I was exploring her communication skills, she asked good questions about the nature of the work. She seemed to really listen to my responses.

Sam: But won't she get bored here? She's already had amazing experience during her research internships. She talked to me about the work she did in the lab with Dr. Makinen. Both the enzyme kinetics, ENDOR spectroscopy, and molecular modeling sounded awfully specialized and not what we might encounter here. I'm afraid our research jobs won't give her the kinds of challenges she might be looking for.

Jane: I worried about that and spoke to her about how she'd felt being lowest on the totem pole as a student intern in a world of high-powered academics. She answered that she has a thirst for learning. I was exploring her problem-solving and goal-setting skills. When we talked about how she goes about setting goals, I got the impression she does a lot of research. She knew an awful lot about our company.

Sam: I wonder whom she talked to. Maybe she gathered information from us when we interviewed her. She asked me a lot of questions about the nature of our research.

Pete: Sam, you didn't say what rating you gave Marsha.

Sam: (Shrugs) I guess I'm off-base compared with the rest of you, but I gave her a 3 because I don't see her fitting in, particularly for the long haul. I suspect she'll stay a few years and then move on. She seems inclined toward teaching.

Pete: I gave her a 3 as well. My concerns, though, had more to do with her presentation. She seemed well versed, but I didn't sense a lot of confidence in what she was saying. Several times when we asked her questions, she had to refer to her notes. That isn't bad in and of itself, but the questions didn't seem that hard. She should have been able to respond off the cuff.

Jane: I'm sure she was a bit nervous. Everyone is.

Pete: Maybe, but surely she's had to make many difficult presentations. This shouldn't have been that hard for her. And we do need someone who can perform at that level.

Lonny: I did talk to her about her leadership positions. We spent most of our time talking about her work with undergrads in Chicago. Apparently she enjoyed that work so much she began tutoring privately. She even taught violin students. I got the impression she really enjoys the teaching role.

Jane: We talked about those experiences as well. She seemed pretty proud of the way her students performed. I suspect she's a very good teacher, very patient and a good listener. I asked her to share instances where the students didn't live up to her expectations. She couldn't come up with anything too specific.

Lonny: There's no question Marsha would make an excellent researcher. The question seems to be how long she'd be happy doing strictly research. When I gave her a 2, I hadn't really thought about that.

Sam: I think Marsha is a great candidate. She's certainly got all the skills we're looking for. I think her presentation skills will improve with time. I thought she was very personable and easy to talk to. But I have too many concerns about whether or not she would be happy with us. I see her moving into an academic position where she can do research and also teach. I suspect she'll be gone in less than a year, and we'll be back to the drawing board.

Jane: I sure hate for the company to lose her.

Lonny: I second that, but I think we've got to think of the longer term. From what Sam says and you, too, Pete, I agree. I suggest we don't make her an offer.

Pete: Do we have consensus?

Sam: I agree with Lonny.

Jane: I hate it, but I think you guys are probably right.

Pete: That's it then. Let's look at the next candidate.

Did you sense groupthink going on here? When groupthink happens, everyone agrees and there's no disagreement. I did not sense that with this group. Let's look at how this group avoided the groupthink trap:

• First, each person had a chance to talk about how he or she felt about the candidate *before* the group leader spoke. We don't know if Pete is a higher-level manager than the others, but as group leader, his opinion carries more weight regardless of his actual position. He waited until everyone had a say before he jumped in.

• Second, the group gave a numerical ranking to the candidate. The numbers alone mean nothing, but they are a quick way to isolate how individuals feel about a candidate. Furthermore, giving numeric scores forces members to come up with an individual decision. Pete asked them to do this before anyone spoke. Notice Sam did not want to share his numerical ranking because he felt out of sync with the others. Pete asked him to do so. That request enabled Sam to share his concerns, which turned out to be vital to the final decision.

INTERVIEW PROCESS EFFECTIVENESS ASSESSMENT

1. Who are the people most affected by this vacant position? Are these people part of your interview team?

2. Did your team study the résumés and applications separately or together?

3. Did your team examine the position and identify the organizational culture?

4. Did your team identify the qualities needed to successfully perform the functions of this position?

5. How many people within your organization need to interview this candidate? If more than eight, did your team organize and plan team or panel interviews?

6. What visual messages about your organization did you want to send? How did you set up ways for the candidate to experience those messages?

7. Did someone in your organization make contact with the candidates to give them directions and make arrangements for the visit?

8. Did your team avoid asking similar questions by focusing on particular areas and by tagging each other at the end of interviews to help build consistency from one interview to the next?

9. Did team members refrain from sharing their impressions as they escorted the candidate from one interviewer to the next?

10. Did interviewers avoid interviewing the candidate around meals?

11. Did the candidates have a chance to visit with people they will supervise?

12. Did the candidates have a chance to visit with peers?

13. Were the interviews conducted in a timely fashion?

Finally, as we've seen in this chapter to apply the "test" in the POINT process, you must examine more than the candidate and his fit in the organization. You must examine yourself and others as interviewers; that is, did you perform competent and careful strategic interviews? You must also examine the interviewing and recruiting process, that is, what happened to the candidates from the time they walked through the door to the final decision meeting. These kinds of evaluations, along with other tools such as skills tests and references, put you in a good position to make that final decision of whom to hire.

PRACTICE EXERCISE

Read the following interview and, using the Interviewer Effectiveness Assessment, rate this interviewer.

Interviewer: Good morning. Thank you for coming in today. My name is Jake, and I'll be talking to you first. Then Mark from our retail division will talk to you. I hope you didn't have any trouble finding us.

Candidate: A little, but I figured it out. It's a little confusing around the circle.

Interviewer: Yes, everyone gets lost there. What made you decide to apply for the sales clerk position?

Candidate: I wanted to work nearby, and I've had a lot of experience as a sales clerk. The job looked interesting, so I thought I'd give it a shot.

Interviewer: What kinds of things are you looking for in a job?

Candidate: I want something regular that I can depend on, and I want to be able to come to work close by so I don't have to drive far. I also want to work in a busy place. I don't like being bored.

Interviewer: Do you have trouble working different hours?

Candidate: No, I'm fine with that. I've worked shifts a lot in my other jobs.

Interviewer: What about weekend work? Do you mind that?

Candidate: Not at all.

How would you grade this interviewer: A, B, C, D, or F?
See Appendix A for an analysis of this interview.

ELEVEN

Sticky Situations in an Interview

We have reached a point in this book where we've presented, discussed, and practiced all the skills necessary to conduct a strategic interview using POINT. We've examined the pros and cons for team interviewing and for behavior-based questioning. We've looked at the importance of staying legal in an interview. Having done all this, it is time for you to embark on your first strategic interview. Before you make that leap, however, we want to prepare you for whatever sticky situations you may encounter in the interview environment.

In this chapter we will explore some of the more difficult situations you may face as a strategic interviewer. Even with all the new skills you've learned, you will face times when carrying out a strategic interview is hard. Sometimes candidates talk too much and it is hard for you to get a word in, much less listen to every word she says. The flipside is when candidates do not talk at all and even when you do all you can to open the candidate up, he stays quiet. At other times you sit face to face with a candidate whom you clearly do not like or who clearly does not like you. All these kinds of situations cause even the best strategic interviewers to pause and scratch their heads in frustration.

There is no requirement that says you must hire everyone you interview, but you do want those people you see to leave feeling as though they had a fair shot. But when it is clear that the person will not fit your job, why can't you simply end the interview and go on to the next? What difference does it make if the candidate feels slighted or out of sorts?

These are good questions. You can indeed end the interview, but the problem comes with trying to extricate yourself in a professional manner. You represent your company or organization. Every person you see will leave with some idea, good or bad, about your company. Even if you know you will not hire the individual, you want to handle the interview professionally. Good interviews are easy to handle professionally. It's the bad interviews—the ones that require all our skills in diplomacy—that are harder. Believe me, it is not professional to begin an interview and in your next breath say, "Thanks for coming. We'll be in touch." In this chapter we will give you some tips for dealing with those kinds of sticky situations to enable you to conduct all interviews in a professional manner.

STICKY INTERVIEW SITUATION 1: CANDIDATE TALKS TOO MUCH

Interviewer: Thank you for coming in today to talk about the sales management position with Zebra Products. My name is Janice, and I work as part of the Zebra sales team.

Candidate: I am so happy to meet you. I've wanted to work for this company my entire life. I heard about Zebra Products when I was growing up and always admired what you guys do. It's amazing to be in this office and even sitting here and talking to you. My heart is aflutter. I've had lots of experience in sales, mostly with pharmaceuticals. I worked for one of the largest pharmaceutical companies in the country for five years. It was great experience for me being able to learn the ropes of selling and meeting so many people—

Interviewer: Let me ask you right quick. What it is about Zebra Products that you admire so—?

Candidate: Oh my gosh! Everything. What isn't there to admire? I mean, you guys take such care with everything. It must be very easy to sell your products. Your salespeople hardly have to do anything 'cause the reputation is so high. And sometimes with the pharmaceutical company I worked for, I didn't always understand what the drug did. It was hard reading all about them and trying to keep up. I did it, and I enjoyed the work, but I often had to struggle. I don't see that with Zebra. In fact, I know a lot about the products you sell because I've used them all my life. Everything from the soap I use in the bathroom to my dish detergent. It's not a hard thing to sell at all—unlike a drug that is supposed to suppress your immune system or something like that.

Interviewer: Our products are not as complicated as drugs, certainly. But we do have a large research team that develops some of the best—

Candidate: Of course, I didn't mean to imply that Zebra products weren't tested or anything like that. I just meant that it wouldn't take as long to understand the ins and outs, so to speak.

Interviewer: Our sales jobs require a lot of travel. My guess is you travelled a lot with the drug company and that might not—

Candidate:	Absolutely no problem. I love to travel and see parts of the country I might not get to see otherwise, and it's a great way to meet people. I've meet so many people working as a drug rep. I learned all the doctor's names and their staff. It's a great way to spend the day—meeting people, taking them to lunch, and visiting with them. You find out so much about all kinds of people all over the country.
Interviewer:	I know traveling is great, but it has its drawbacks. What are some of the difficulties you faced with a job that is primarily on the road?
Candidate:	I really can't think of a single one. Well, once I was sick and I really didn't feel like getting up. I was in a hotel. It's not fun being sick when you're in a hotel. When you're sick you want your own bed and all. That's about the only thing I can think of.

Let's look at what the interviewer had to do to maintain a professional interview.

- The interviewer continued to jump in with key questions, even though she had to interrupt the candidate a couple of times (and many times she was interrupted).
- The interviewer did not give up and sit back and simply listen.
- The interviewer used the intentional listening skills to pull out the important components to help her understand what she needed.
- The interviewer listened but did not piggy-back or use skills to keep the candidate talking.

Remember, there is nothing illegal in listening. This interviewer learned a lot about this candidate by listening to the chatter. First, the candidate talked so much that it would be hard for her to make a sale. How could the candidate learn what a customer wanted if she talked all the time? Second, this candidate loved the company's products but did not appreciate their depth. Third, this candidate had a romantic view of travelling without a good understanding of the sacrifices. Indeed, you may doubt that Janice would offer this candidate a job. But when the candidate leaves the interview, she will have a good impression of Janice, and her view of the company will not diminish.

STICKY INTERVIEW SITUATION 2: CANDIDATE DOESN'T TALK ENOUGH

Interviewer:	Good afternoon, Mr. Patterson, my name is Lou Jones, and I am the shift supervisor. I'll be talking to you a few minutes this afternoon before we take you on a tour. May I call you Jeff?

Jeff:	Sure.
Lou:	Great, Jeff. I must say I was impressed by your résumé. You've had some awesome experience in the field of management. So tell me, what attracted you to our company?
Jeff:	The location.
Lou:	I take it you want to work in the Chicago area?
Jeff:	That's right.
Lou:	I can relate to that. I grew up just a few miles from here. It's a great location. Not in the city, but close enough. I love the opportunity to come into town for sports events but then get back home in 20 minutes.
Jeff:	(Nods but says nothing)
Lou:	What is it about this location that you appreciate?
Jeff:	Just what you said.
Lou:	All right. So tell me, Jeff, I noticed that you play tennis. I'm a great tennis fan. I can't play anymore because my knees gave out on me. But I do love watching. What do you like about the sport?
Jeff:	Being able to play singles.
Lou:	What is it about singles you like better than doubles?
Jeff:	I like hitting lots of balls and not depending on a partner.
Lou:	Tennis is a pretty competitive sport. How competitive a person are you?
Jeff:	Enough, I guess.
Lou:	How about sharing an example in your career when you were competitive?
Jeff:	Landing my last job.
Lou:	So you had to be competitive to land your job?
Jeff:	Yeah, there were lots of candidates.
Lou:	What did you have to do to land your last job?
Jeff:	I suppose I did what I needed to do to beat everyone out.
Lou:	Yes, I agree. Landing a job feels like winning, like in a tennis match. You've been with Mercurial Inc. for three years. What made you decide to look elsewhere?
Jeff:	It was time and, like I said, I like the location.
Lou:	You've got quite a large team working under you—30 people. How do you manage that team?
Jeff:	They pretty much manage themselves.
Lou:	So are you saying you have a negligible role with your team?
Jeff:	Like I say, they manage themselves.
Lou:	So, what is your role with the team?

Jeff:	(Silence) I suppose I just keep things moving.
Lou:	Share an example of what that looks like—how you keep things moving.
Jeff:	When things bog down, they call on me. That's about it.
Lou:	We've got a pretty large operation here that requires round-the-clock attention. Our teams are self-managed as well. But we do require regular meetings and good communication across boundaries. How did you manage communication across the various units?
Jeff:	Mostly, people talk informally.

Lou struggled to get information out of Jeff Patterson. It was difficult to tell whether Jeff was simply a taciturn person or if he was deliberately holding back. Let's look at what Lou did to try to get Jeff to open up.

- He began the interview graciously and on a first-name basis.
- He complimented Jeff's career experience.
- He shared information about himself several times: first when he talked about the location of the company and second when he talked about his experience with tennis.
- He shared information about the company.
- He did not simply probe, but he paraphrased a few times and even tried a flipside and a reality test. If he had simply probed and the candidate felt cross-examined, he might have clammed up more.
- He avoided asking closed questions unless absolutely necessary.
- He did not give up.

We doubt very seriously that Lou will hire Jeff. If, however, Lou continues the interview, sharing about himself and the company and learning small tidbits about Jeff, the candidate will exit the interview feeling as though he had a quality interview. If Lou gives up and begins asking closed questions, and his nonverbal cues show his frustration, Jeff will exit the interview with negative feelings about Lou and the company.

Even if Jeff's lack of conversation had not been a problem for Lou, some of the things Jeff said potentially ruined his chance of getting hired. When he responded that he liked to play singles tennis because he didn't like to depend on a partner, he put up a big red flag for someone interviewing for a managerial position. Furthermore, his admitted competitiveness might pose a problem, depending on the job. Lou never got Jeff to open up. At some point in the interview, the goal to create openness fell away, and a new goal emerged: get through the interview on a positive note.

STICKY INTERVIEW SITUATIONS 3: CANDIDATE ON A TOUR ASKS PERSONAL QUESTIONS

Emily Jamison is taking Mary Lou Smith on a tour of the company's facilities.

Emily: This is just one of the floors full of cubicles where most of our employees work. We have six floors.

Mary Lou: It's amazing to see people working in cubicles. The cubicle generation took off after I left the workforce in the 1990s. People look happy enough, and I see photos of children and pets. Do you have any kids? (They move along the corridor and observe people on telephones or working at their desks.)

Emily: Yes, actually, I have two kids. This is our sales floor. Most of the people you see are busy selling radio time or ads for the newspaper.

Mary Lou: How old are your kids?

Emily: Nine and eleven. I'd like you to meet our director of sales. (She introduces Mary Lou to the director, and they talk briefly before moving on.)

Mary Lou: It must be hard for you to leave your kids to go to work. I couldn't do it. That's why I left the workforce. I wanted to be a stay-at-home mom, so I devoted my time to my kids. I once told a friend, "They are my job now." I'll never regret that. But as I look at the modern work world, it's daunting. So much has changed since I left in the mid-1990s. (Emily doesn't respond. They enter the elevator and travel to another floor.)

Mary Lou: (Inside the elevator) What do moms with kids do when a child gets sick at school? Do y'all mind if they leave?

Emily: We have a very flexible work schedule. Some of our employees opt to work at home; others work odd hours. For example, some come in very early in the morning and leave right before lunch. That's one of the beauties about working here. (Off the elevator, they move down a long corridor.)

Emily: This is the corporate floor. Over there is the main conference room where the board meets once a month. (They enter a large room, beautifully furnished.)

Mary Lou: Gosh, this is amazing. I'm sure I'd never have to come up here for anything. Where is everyone, by the way?

Emily: Actually, most of the staff give regular reports right here in this room several times a year. You would, too, if you're hired. It's really not that bad; everyone supports you. As far as where everyone is today, the corporate team is off on an assignment in town. They should be back first thing tomorrow. Now, let's head down to the basement, where you'll see a lot of people busy getting out today's edition.

Mary Lou: When I worked in a local paper during school, there were very few women in the top positions. I suppose all that has changed. How hard is it for a woman to move up in this company?

Emily: We've got a number of women in editorial positions. From my experience, if you do a good job, you'll get positive recognition and rewards. That's all anyone could ask for. (They reach the basement, where lots of activity is going on—many people milling about.)

Mary Lou: I'm still blown away by the changes. Everyone has computers. What are all of them doing?

Emily: Most are entering blog posts. We follow and add content to may news blogs. We also have our own internal and external blogs.

Mary Lou: I've got so much to learn. (She laughs nervously.) I'm not really sure what a blog is. You seem so young. I've probably been out of the workforce longer than you've been in it. Is there a problem with hiring seasoned people like me? Everyone I've seen so far looks so young.

Emily: (Laughs off Mary Lou's comment) We all had lots to learn when we were initially hired. Our goal is to hire the best candidates for our jobs. Now come this way—I'd like you to meet some people in our productions department. They're in the break room. (After they spend a brief time talking to people in the break room, Emily ushers Mary Lou back to the lobby to collect her things.)

Emily: I enjoyed meeting you today and having an opportunity to show you around. We are interviewing several more candidates this afternoon and tomorrow. Once we complete that process, we will let you know our decision. Thank you for coming in and, again, for the opportunity to meet you.

Mary Lou: I appreciate everything you've done. Thank you. (They shake hands before departing.)

The general informality of tours makes them one of the best places to build rapport and one of the most dangerous places for loose chatter. Mary Lou shared a lot of information about herself—information that would be considered illegal in a traditional interview. She tried to pull Emily in by asking her questions about her children and about her age. Let's look at what Emily did to keep from getting drawn in.

• She quickly answered the questions Mary Lou asked. She didn't answer all of them, but she answered enough to appear polite.

- She deflected her questions by stopping to introduce her to people along the way.
- She kept the tour moving without stopping to chatter.
- When questions appeared very dangerous, she didn't answer or changed the subject.
- When she could, she sprinkled information about the job (flexible hours; rewarding people, male and female, for good work; hiring the best).
- At the end of the tour, she walked Mary Lou out and thanked her for coming in. She also told her when they would be in touch. She did not ask if she had additional questions. With a candidate like Mary Lou, you would not want to solicit more questions. With other candidates, you might.

STICKY INTERVIEW SITUATION 4: A CANDIDATE STEPS OVER THE LINE

Interviewer: Good morning, Mr. Sams. My name is Marcy Marino. I'm the director of administration and will be starting off your interviews today. You've got a full day ahead of you, so we'll get started. Please call me Marcy, and if I may call you Robert?

Robert: Absolutely, Marcy. (He smiles and leans in)

Marcy: You've lived a long time on the West Coast. I'm from Seattle and love that part of the country. How has it been adjusting to the Midwest?

Robert: I could tell you were not from here. You seem much too, let's say, warm and personable, to have been a Midwestern girl. They're all so unapproachable.

Marcy: So you've noticed a difference in people from this part of the country?

Robert: My goodness, yes. The women are so hardnosed, if you know what I mean. They're as stiff as boards, never smile, and can't take a joke. I'm divorced and am interested in finding a partner. Out here it isn't easy.

Marcy: What about the people you manage—have you noticed differences there as well?

Robert: If you mean the line crew, yes, I have. In California everything is relaxed. People go out for drinks together. My God, we went skinny dipping in the Pacific. (He grins at her.) But Oklahoma is just like the songs—very traditional. I've had to adjust.

Marcy: So how have you adjusted?

Robert: (He leans further in and uncrosses his legs.) I stay alert for my kind of people, like you, Marcy, and I'm real clear about it when I see it.

Marcy:	Tell me more about your role as shift supervisor with Mills Hospital.
Robert:	(Settles back in his seat) I seem to have offended you. I apologize. I can be rather direct sometimes, particularly when I see something I like. Let's see, my role as shift supervisor. I'm in charge of the output of the team. I have a team of 15 transcriptionists. They have grueling jobs. I try to be sympathetic with them, but it's hard. There's lots of gossiping and complaining. That's the nature of the beast, I guess. I am looking to find a place that is more positive— where people don't have to gripe all the time to get by.
Marcy:	It sounds as if the office environment in your current job frustrates you.
Robert:	Oh yes, it does. No matter what I do to make their lives easier, there are gripes. But I'm hoping to leave all that behind me. (He smiles again and gives her direct eye contact.)
Marcy:	Give me an example of what you tried to do to make their lives easier.
Robert:	(Sighs) I got the hours changed to enable them to have more free time. I started a rewards program to recognize my best performers. (Sighs) I encouraged them to do things together —get to know one another on a personal basis. That always helps in my opinion. After my divorce, one of my coworkers was very supportive. She got me through the tough times and the lonely times. It was especially hard for me to move away from my kids. Do you have any kids?
Marcy:	No, I don't. When your coworkers did not respond to all you did for them, what did you do?
Robert:	I guess I started tuning out their complaints. My goal now is to get through the day and let them be.
Marcy:	It must have been disappointing to you for them to continue to complain even though you were doing all you could for them.
Robert:	It was, but I realized I couldn't do anything about it. Some environments fester with complaining. That's how they thrive. I was fighting a losing battle.
Marcy:	What do you mean by fighting a losing battle?
Robert:	I realized that the culture was one of complaining to get by. It had gone on long before I got there and it will continue long after I leave. It's going to take more than me to change it.
Marcy:	Give me an instance when you realized that this was a cultural problem.

Here we have a candidate with a full day of interviews scheduled. Marcy knows immediately that she is not going to recommend this candidate for hire. He has acted unprofessionally in the interview in several ways: (1) he openly flirted with her, (2) he seemed bothered to be answering her questions about his work, and (3) he stereotyped people. Nonetheless, Marcy must continue the interview in as professional a manner as possible and not voice her concerns to her colleagues. Marcy's first thought might be, "Why waste everyone's time by interviewing this man?" One reason for doing so, however, is he went through the company's careful screening process and something about him suggested he might be a valuable candidate. She must allow her colleagues to draw their own conclusions. She can voice her concerns during the assessment meeting at the end. Meantime, let's look at what Marcy did during the interview.

- She began her interview with an icebreaker to create trust with the candidate. It did not take long for her to realize she had to move into the heart of the interview. She was on dangerous ground with this candidate.
- When the candidate openly flirted with her or said inappropriate things, she continued to focus the interview on work-related questions. She did not acknowledge the candidate when he said, "I seem to have offended you." She let that pass and proceeded with her questions.
- The candidate asked her about her children and shared information about his personal life, but she refrained from falling into that trap.
- She did not end the interview abruptly (although she may have wanted to). Instead she continued to explore the candidate's relationship with his staff and his management style.
- Toward the end of the interview, she kept control by focusing on his behaviors as a manager. She reflected his feelings a couple of times. You might wonder why reflection worked in this situation. Reflection is often used to build trust and rapport. In all likelihood Marcy didn't wish to build trust and rapport with this candidate. But because Robert seemed a very insecure person who used flirtation to maintain distance, Marcy gently reflected in order to chip away at the insecurity.

In this chapter we examined four sticky situations in interviews. We looked at how to use the POINT process to enable you to conduct difficult interviews professionally. Knowing the purpose of each of the intentional listening skills enables savvy interviewers to extricate themselves from sticky interview situations in a manner that leaves the candidate feeling positive.

Chapter 12 will conclude with some additional tips for how to keep the people you finally decide to hire.

TWELVE

Hire Smart and Keep 'Em: Retaining Your Best Hires

So far in this book we've stressed the skills for conducting a strategic interview using POINT. We've examined how to *Plan* your recruiting process and interviews; we've looked at the importance of creating trust and keeping your interviews *Open*; we've examined the skills (*Intentional Listening*) necessary to dig deeply and uncover truths beyond the superficial. And we've looked at *Testing* and constantly tweaking yourself as an interviewer as well as the process itself. All these efforts will enable you to become a skilled strategic interviewer who knows how to hire smart. If you apply the skills in this book, you will learn enough information to make a good decision that plays into retention. But there is more to keeping 'em than meets the eye.

In this chapter we will take a look at some of the factors you need to consider when thinking about staying power. You want to hire smart, which means finding people who fit your job requirements, but you also want to keep them, and that means doing a bit more.

HONESTY IS THE BEST POLICY

When you were 10 years old, I know you were told to always tell the truth. Being honest is as important today as it was then. We mentioned earlier in this book that part of creating trust is being open and honest. This maxim applies to you as much as it does to the candidate. At times you must let prospective hires know about the blemishes in your organization. I don't mean sitting there and griping about this and that. You don't want to appear to be airing dirty laundry. Nonetheless, it is important to let the candidate know what challenges she will face. Let's look at an example:

Candidate: Tell me about the people I will be supervising.

Interviewer: You have five direct reports. They each have a department they manage. Two of your direct reports have been with this organization for over 20 years. Neither shows any signs of retiring. The other three are newer. I will say that it's been a challenge to turn these people into a solid team. They seem too turf conscious to be interested in the good of the whole.

Candidate: I noticed that the division leaders that have been here in the past have not stayed too long. What happened to make them leave?

Interviewer: Each left for different reasons. One person wanted to return to finish her MBA. After that, we hired someone in that job, but he only stayed a couple of years. He was essentially over his head. He had trouble building communication across the departmental lines. When he was offered a job somewhere else, he took it.

Candidate: So is it the staff challenges that seem to cause frustration on the leader's part?

Interviewer: That's what we are seeing. I want you to understand the challenge here, but, if we hire you, we will give you all the help we can. I believe the five individuals are anxious to have good solid leadership; they are rudderless now. Each has done a good job with his or her individual department and has unique talent and skill. But there's no question changes need to be made. Whomever we hire in this job will have our support in whatever that person decides to do to make this division function successfully. And we are looking for a candidate whom we feel has the skill to turn things around. That was one reason we wanted to interview you.

In this example the candidate got an honest assessment of the challenges in the job. The interviewer neither tried to diminish the issues nor dwelled on negativity. He pointed out the opportunities within the challenge. Furthermore, he made it sound as though one reason they might hire this candidate is their confidence she can handle the challenge.

Note also that as an interviewer you learn a lot from the questions candidates ask about the challenges in the job. The candidate in this example seemed to want to hear what the interviewer had to say and appeared to understand the real issues. She did not shrink away from the potential difficulties the interviewer presented.

ENCOURAGE CANDIDATES TO INTERVIEW YOU

We've talked a lot about trying to get beyond the superficial and getting candidates to tell you something they didn't intend to tell you, the point being that most candidates want to make the hiring decision alone. You, too, want to make the decision alone. The need to keep things hidden on both sides of the table creates major dissonance. As a manager who wants to retain the people you hire, you want to close that gap as much as possible. By giving candidates a chance to ask you questions and by responding in an open and honest way, you enable them to probe your hidden area. *When both sides use the skills in this book, the likelihood of hiring smart and keeping 'em increases.* Unfortunately, most candidates do not want to appear too probing. They worry if they ask too many questions or if their questions probe too deeply, they won't get an offer. As an interviewer, you want to encourage them to open up and ask the questions that might help them make an educated decision. Let's look an example:

Candidate:	One of my goals is to complete my graduate degree in the next five years. Tell me more about this company's position on education.
Interviewer:	As I've said, you will be encouraged to take classes on your own time. We've had a number of people in the company complete MBAs while working for us. Although we do not pay for someone's professional education, we do encourage people to go to school.
Candidate:	When you say you encourage people to go to school, what do you mean?
Interviewer:	As long as the job gets done up to standards, we do not hold people to rigid schedules. Let's say you have a late afternoon class and must leave by 4 p.m. If your work is done, we do not frown upon your leaving for class. We expect you to put your work objectives above your educational objectives. But we do not stand in the way of our employees who want to get professional degrees.
Candidate:	So it's possible for someone in my position to take a course during the workday?
Interviewer:	Indeed, so as long as it does not disrupt your work.
Candidate:	In what other ways do you encourage people who might be pursuing a professional degree?

In this case, the candidate sought enough information to get a good idea about whether or not this company would enable him to return to school. He learned that the company provided no financial help with higher education but that he could take classes during the workday. Nonetheless, he must fulfill the work goals and make education a lesser priority to work. If this candidate places a higher priority on education than work, this might not be the best company for him. He might search for a job of lesser importance—a part-time job, perhaps. This is something the candidate must determine. Let's examine another example where the candidate is more reluctant to ask questions.

Interviewer: I've told you a lot about the company and our opening. I'm sure you've got some questions for me.

Candidate: (Nods) As you know, I want to stay with this company for as long as possible. I'm curious about the opportunities to promote from within.

Interviewer: We always try to promote our own people, but we do not exclusively promote from within. We value new ideas that come with outside hires. It's a balancing act. But there have been many instances where our current employees have had the talent and skills to move up and we've promoted them.

Candidate: That's great. Thank you for sharing that.

Interviewer: What other questions do you have, either about internal promotions or anything else?

Candidate: You did a great job sharing with me. I understand a lot about your company and the requirements of this job.

Interviewer: From what I told you, is there anything that might cause you to pause before accepting an offer? Anything at all?

Candidate: The only thing that might be a problem is what you said about orientation to the different shifts. You told me that new hires work all the shifts. I realize that it's important for new people to learn the organization and how the shifts work, but that might be a problem for me. I'm sure there are some exceptions to this rule.

Interviewer: Perhaps we have made a few exceptions, but not often. And you're right, the adjustment to the different shifts is hard, but most of us got used to it after a week or so. I really enjoyed the night-shift crew. They are such a different breed. I could have never gotten to know them the way I did had I not worked several months on that shift.

Candidate: I really like what you've told me about the job and the company. I think I'd fit in well here.

Interviewer: Just so you understand, the policy about working the different shifts for the first year of employment is pretty strict. I've only known of one exception while I've been here. That was for a woman whose husband was wheelchair bound, and she was his primary caretaker. He needed her in the house at night with him. As far as I know the company never exempted anyone else, even people with small children and

	other kinds of responsibilities from this part of the orientation.
Candidate:	Thank you for sharing that. But I don't think it will be a problem. I'll learn to adjust and perhaps, like you, find I like the different shifts.

This interviewer might have stopped probing after the initial invitation to ask questions. Instead, she pushed a bit harder until the candidate felt more comfortable exploring some areas that might cause a problem if she was hired. Nonetheless, the candidate did not probe too hard. She asked one question and stopped. The interviewer took the initiative to add more information. If the interviewer felt there was too much hesitancy on the part of the candidate, she might decide not to hire. Meantime, the candidate left with a clear understanding that she would have to work odd shifts for her first year of employment. She did not leave believing she could get out of this requirement.

GOOD MANAGEMENT

Good management and leadership go beyond the scope of this book. I would be remiss, however, if I did not mention the importance of these factors in keeping quality talent. You and your hiring team might do everything right from the initial contact to the final interviews and the decision to hire, but you may still experience high turnover. When that happens, it may not be the hiring machine that is broken; it may be something else. Take a look at your communication channels. Take a look at your reward system. Take a look at your management team.

Some years ago, a director of an organization called me in to consult with his team. Before I began talking to people to discover where the problems were, he said, "I hope I'm not the problem." Of course, as it turned out, he was the primary problem. He micromanaged his staff and lost his temper when they didn't perform up to his expectations. He hired talented, creative people whom he placed in a box, never allowing them to blossom. This caused frustration in the team and high turnover. *If you hire creative people, you must let them create.* If you hire someone with the clear challenge to increase productivity, you must give that person the latitude to accomplish that goal. Otherwise, hire people who will do nothing more than what you want them to do. There may be instances when hiring followers is what you want. Make sure, however, that you find people that fit that niche.

Another organization where I consulted liked to hire people with the highest leadership potential. The CEO said, "We're a top-notch company; we want top-notch people." The problem was the jobs were not challenging. The jobs required people with high energy but little creativity. Smart human resources professionals recognized this and hired people that fit the jobs rather than people the CEO liked. You can be a top-notch company with a lot of worker bees. Not everyone needs to lead.

If you have a situation where poor management or leadership prevails, but you must hire people to work for these poor leaders, think about the people who have successfully worked for them in the past. What did they do to succeed, and what skills did they have? You may have to change your target competencies to fit the environment in which the person will be working.

TO SUMMARIZE

To hire smart and keep 'em takes good strategic interviewing using the POINT process. It also takes consideration of the job and the environment where the person will be working. If you work in a highly competitive environment, for example, you must find people whose past behavior has shown that they can survive in a highly competitive environment. I once had a client who indeed had worked in such an environment and had been successful. But she hated it. She left that environment to find something less stressful. In a situation like this the interviewer can't simply look at past behavior but must also dig deeper to determine what the candidate wants in a job.

If you are honest, encourage the candidate to interview you, and take your own management issues into consideration, your chances of hiring people who will stay will increase.

The goal of any interviewer is to hire successfully at least 80 percent of the time. Remember the only true measure of success in a job is actually doing the job. Interviews do not enable you to observe a person in the job. They only give you information to help you determine if the person can *likely* perform. You expect to make mistakes. But if you make mistakes more than 20 percent of the time, you are not hiring smart.

This book contains the skills necessary to hire smart and keep 'em. If you practice what I've outlined here, you will become a savvy strategic interviewer who will achieve at least 80 percent success and fewer costly hiring mistakes. This book primes you to tackle the challenge of hiring smart every time. You are now equipped with the skills to hire the right people on your team. You now know *how to do it.*

What are you waiting for? It's time for you to experience the joy of interviewing and the pleasure of seeing people working in jobs they enjoy.

APPENDIX A

Answers to Practice Exercises

CHAPTER 1

The interview was laissez faire

CHAPTER 2

1. False
2. True
3. False
4. False
5. False
6. False
7. True
8. False

CHAPTER 3

Numbers 1, 6, 9, and 10 are behavior based.

CHAPTER 4

1. b
2. c
3. e

4. d

5. a

6. b

7. d

8. c

CHAPTER 5

Those that apply:

1. The interviewer asked questions that related to age (not directly, but implied).
6. The interviewer asked questions related to religion (not directly, but implied).

If there's a violation of any one of the items on the list, the interview is not considered legal. This interview could be contested even though no direct illegal questions were asked.

CHAPTER 6

1. False

2. False

3. True

4. False

5. False

CHAPTER 7

1. b

2. b

3. a

4. c

5. b

6. c

7. b

8. c

9. a
10. c

CHAPTER 8

1. Probe responses
    a. Give me an example of a challenging situation you had in your last job.
    b. How do you see Sanders Company as being progressive?
    c. Tell me what you did as spokesperson for the team.
    d. How did you attempt to deal with your boss before you left?
        (There are many different ways to construct probes to these responses. Check to see if you piggy-backed your response and created an open question).
2. Paraphrase responses
    a. In other words, your last job didn't impose a lot of restrictions?
    b. Are you saying you prefer working with people to doing tasks solo?
    c. Am I clear that your vacation time is very important to you?
    d. Traveling is hard for you, right?
        (There are many different ways to construct a paraphrase to these responses.)
3. Flipside response: That team experience sounded very rewarding to you. Describe the challenges you experienced in working with so large a team. (There are many different ways to construct a flipside to this response.)

CHAPTER 9

1. Summary response: Let me try and summarize. You began in sales and, although you enjoyed it, you needed more challenge, and that's how you ended up in a teaching role. (There are many different ways to construct a summary statement to this response.)
2. Reality-test response
    a. Are you saying that even though you've never experienced team-work, you would enjoy it?
    b. Let me see if I'm clear—you don't mind working as much as 80 hours a week?
        (There are many different ways to construct a reality test for these responses.)

3. Reflection response
   a. It sounds like routine work tires you.
   b. So the night shift might overwhelm you?
   c. Wow! You sound proud of that accomplishment.
   d. You were surprised she felt that way?
      (There are many was to construct a reflection. Make sure you capture a feeling.)

CHAPTER 10

I gave this interview a D.

The main problem with this interview was asking closed questions. The interviewer's plan might have been to learn what kind of job the candidate was looking for, but he didn't find that out by asking closed questions. He had a decent opening but not much of an icebreaker. The candidate never opened up.

Furthermore, when the interviewer did "react," he only probed. Otherwise, he didn't use any other intentional listening skill.

APPENDIX B

Action Verbs

The following list of action verbs is not exhaustive. It will, however, give you an idea of what an action verb is and help you select one for your job descriptions.

Accelerated

Accomplished

Achieved

Acquired

Acted

Activated

Adapted

Addressed

Adjusted

Administered

Advanced

Advertised

Advised

Advocated

Allocated

Analyzed

Answered

Applied

Appointed

Appraised

Arranged

Boosted

Briefed

Budgeted

Built

Calculated

Captured

Cataloged

Chaired

Championed

Charted

Checked

Clarified

Classified

Coached

Coded
Collected
Communicated
Compared
Compiled
Composed
Computed
Condensed
Conducted
Conferred
Constructed
Consulted
Contacted
Contracted
Controlled
Converted
Conveyed
Convinced
Coordinated
Corrected
Corresponded
Counseled
Crafted
Created
Critiqued

Debated
Debugged
Decided
Defined
Delegated
Delivered
Demonstrated
Designated
Designed

Determined
Developed
Devised
Diagnosed
Directed
Discovered
Discussed
Dispensed
Displayed
Distributed
Documented
Drafted

Earned
Edited
Elected
Elicited
Eliminated
Employed
Enacted
Enforced
Engineered
Enhanced
Enlarged
Enlisted
Established
Estimated
Evaluated
Examined
Executed
Exhibited
Expanded
Expedited
Explained
Explored

Expressed
Extracted

Fabricated
Facilitated
Filed
Finalized
Financed
Fixed
Focused
Forecasted
Formed
Formulated
Fostered
Found
Fulfilled
Furnished

Gained
Gathered
Generated
Governed
Grossed
Guided

Halted
Handled
Headed
Heightened
Hired
Honed
Hosted

Identified
Illustrated
Implemented

Improved
Improvised
Incorporated
Increased
Indexed
Informed
Initiated
Innovated
Inspected
Installed
Instituted
Instructed
Interacted
Interpreted
Intervened
Interviewed
Introduced

Joined
Judged
Jammed

Keynoted
Kibitzed

Launched
Lectured
Led
Lifted
Located
Logged

Managed
Manufactured
Mapped
Marketed

Masterminded

Maximized

Measured

Mediated

Mentored

Merged

Mobilized

Modeled

Moderated

Modified

Monitored

Negotiated

Netted

Nudged

Observed

Obtained

Opened

Operated

Orchestrated

Ordered

Organized

Originated

Outlined

Outsourced

Overcame

Overhauled

Oversaw

Participated

Performed

Persuaded

Photographed

Piloted

Pinpointed

Pioneered

Placed

Planned

Played

Predicted

Prepared

Prescribed

Presented

Presided

Prevented

Printed

Processed

Procured

Produced

Programmed

Promoted

Proofread

Propelled

Proposed

Proved

Publicized

Purchased

Qualified

Questioned

Raised

Ran

Rated

Reached

Realigned

Realized

Reasoned

Received

Recommended
Reconciled
Recorded
Recruited
Rectified
Recycled
Reduced
Referred
Regained
Registered
Regulated
Rehabilitated
Reinforced
Remodeled
Renegotiated
Reorganized
Repaired
Replaced
Reported
Repositioned
Researched
Reserved
Reshaped
Resolved
Responded
Restored
Restructured
Retrieved
Reviewed
Revised
Routed

Saved
Scheduled
Screened

Searched
Secured
Selected
Separated
Shaped
Shared
Simplified
Sketched
Sold
Solicited
Solved
Sorted
Spearheaded
Specified
Spoke
Sponsored
Staffed
Standardized
Started
Streamlined
Strengthened
Structured
Studied
Suggested
Summarized
Supervised
Supplied
Surpassed
Surveyed
Sustained
Synthesized
Systematized

Tabulated
Targeted

Taught

Terminated

Tested

Tightened

Totaled

Tracked

Traded

Trained

Transcribed

Transferred

Transformed

Transitioned

Translated

Transmitted

Traveled

Troubleshot

Tutored

Uncovered

Undertook

Unified

United

Updated

Upgraded

Utilized

Validated

Verbalized

Verified

Vitalized

Volunteered

Wedged

Weighed

Widened

Withdrew

Won

Worked

Wrote

APPENDIX C

Interviewer's Guide

CHECKLIST FOR P—PLAN

- Review application and résumé. Decide what jobs, education, and experience are relevant to your target job.
- Review your target competencies.
- Determine the probe points you intend to explore.
- Note any gaps on the résumé.
- Decide what you might use as an icebreaker.
- Develop one planned probe question for each target.

CHECKLIST FOR OPENING THE INTERVIEW

- Greet the candidate with your name and a welcome from your company.
- Explain the purpose of the interview:
  - To help the candidate and interviewer get to know one another.
  - To learn how the candidate's experience fits with the potential jobs with your company.
  - To acquaint the candidate with the position and the company
- Describe the interview plan—"We're going to have a conversation."
  - Explain if you'll be taking notes.
  - Encourage the candidate to ask questions as the interview progresses.
- Begin with your icebreaker if you haven't done it right after the greeting.
- Transition from the icebreaker into one of your target competencies.

CHECKLIST FOR CONDUCTING THE INTERVIEW

- Ask your planned probe questions for each target.
- Use your intentional listening skills:
  - Probe
  - Paraphrase
  - Flipside
  - Summary
  - Reality-Test
  - Reflection
- Make sure probes reflect behavior in specific situations in the past.
- Transition using information the candidate gives you (piggy-back).
- Self-disclose at appropriate times.
- Respond to the candidate's questions and use them to transition to your next probe.

CHECKLIST FOR ENDING THE INTERVIEW

- Ask the candidate if he or she has additional questions. Encourage the candidate to question you.
- Thank the candidate for interviewing with your company.
- Explain the next steps the person can expect.

POSTINTERVIEW CHECKLIST

- Test the Candidate
  - How does the candidate score on the target competencies?
  - How does the candidate score in terms of staying power?
  - Use an informal scoring system to rate the candidate as shown in the table at the end of this appendix.
- Rate yourself as an interviewer:
  - What was the interviewer's plan?
  - How much time did the interviewer talk versus listen?
  - How did the icebreaker help the candidate open up?
  - When did the interviewer follow up with intentional listening skills?
  - How did the interviewer react to nonverbal cues?
  - When did the interviewer self-disclose?
  - What could the interviewer do to improve?
  - If you had to grade yourself as an interviewer, what grade would you give (A, B, C, D, or F)?

1	Top 10 percent	A candidate who meets all the target competencies and good staying power.
2	Top 25 percent	A candidate who meets all but one or two of the target competencies but has good staying power.
3	Top 50 percent	A candidate who meets all but one or two of the target competencies and has some question about staying power.
4	Lower 50 percent	A candidate who does not meet the minimum number of target competencies and has questionable staying power.

Notes

INTRODUCTION

1. Martin Yate, *Hiring the Best: A Manager's Guide to Effective Interviewing* (Holbrook, MA: Adams Media1994), 13.

2. Pierre Mornell, *Hiring Smart: How to Predict Winners and Losers in the Incredibly Expensive People-Reading Game* (Berkeley/Toronto: Ten Speed Press, 2003), 5.

3. Joan Curtis, *Strategic Interviewing: Skills and Tactics for Savvy Executives* (Westport, CT: Quorum Books, 2000), 2.

CHAPTER 1

1. Dan Erling, *Match: A Systematic, Sane Process for Hiring the Right Person Every Time* (Hoboken, NJ: John Wiley & Sons, 2011), 14.

2. Lou Adler, *Hire with Your Head: Using Performance-Based Hiring to Build Great Teams* (Hoboken, NJ: John Wiley & Sons, 2007), ix.

3. Richard F. Olson, *Managing the Interview* (New York: John Wiley & Sons, 1980), 8.

4. Joan C. Curtis, *Managing Sticky Situations at Work: Communication Secrets for Success in the Workplace* (Santa Barbara, CA: Praeger, 2009), 1.

5. Albert Mehrabian and Morton Weiner, *Language within Language* (Appleton-Century-Crofts, 1968).

6. BBC Science and Nature, *Human Body Mind Surveys*, http://www.bbc.co.uk/science/humanbody/mind/surveys/smiles/.

7. Malcolm Gladwell, *Blink: The Power of Thinking without Thinking* (New York: Little, Brown and Company, 2005), 39.

8. Curtis, *Strategic Interviewing*, 46.

CHAPTER 2

1. Erling, *Match*.
2. Ibid., 56.
3. Joan C. Curtis and Barbara Giamanco, *The New Handshake: Sales Meets Social Media* (Santa Barbara, CA: Praeger, 2010).
4. Skype and Google Talk (http://www.skype.com or http://www.google.com/talk/) provide the same service and at the time of this writing are essentially free. I will refer to Skype as a general term for all web-based visual communication services.

CHAPTER 3

1. Pierre Mornell, *Hiring Smart*, 9.
2. Ibid., 10.
3. Ibid., 15.
4. Ibid., 187–89.

CHAPTER 4

1. William H. Whyte, *The Organization Man* (New York: Simon & Schuster, 1956).
2. Bruce W. Tuckman, *Conducting Educational Research* (New York: Harcourt Brace Jovanovich, 1972; fifth edition by Wadsworth, 1996).
3. Curtis, *Managing Sticky Situations at Work*, 99.
4. Ibid.
5. Ibid.
6. Ibid.

CHAPTER 5

1. Curtis, *Strategic Interviewing*.
2. See http://www.census.gov/prod/2009pubs/p60-237.pdf.
3. Ibid.
4. See http://www.economist.com/node/15174418, December 2009.
5. See http://www.bls.gov/opub/mlr/2002/05/art1full.pdf.
6. See http://economics.about.com/od/laborinamerica/a/diversity.htm.
7. Olsen, *Managing the Interview*, 115.

CHAPTER 6

1. Joseph Luft and Harrington Ingham, *Of Human Interaction* (Palo Alto, CA: National Press, 1969).

CHAPTER 7

1. Yate, *Hiring the Best*.
2. Mornell, *Hiring Smart*, 68.
3. Olson, *Managing the Interview*, 57.
4. Curtis, *Managing Sticky Situations at Work*, 1.
5. Ibid., 2.

CHAPTER 10

1. Adler, *Hire with Your Head*, 193.
2. Ibid.
3. Erling, *Match*, 75.
4. Adler, *Hire with Your Head*, 85.
5. Mornell, *Hiring Smart!* 128.
6. Curtis, *Strategic Interviewing*, 110–11.
7. Erling, *Match*, 14.
8. Curtis, *Strategic Interviewing*, 111.

Index

About the Author

Joan C. Curtis, EdD, is CEO of Total Communications Coach and is nationally known as a communication specialist. She has conducted seminars and workshops for over 20 years (see www.Totalcommunicationscoach.com). She is the author of *The New Handshake: Sales Meets Social Media*, *Managing Sticky Situations at Work: Communication Secrets for Success in the Workplace* (www.managingstickysituationsatwork.com), and *Strategic Interviewing: Skills and Tactics for Savvy Executives*. She has won numerous awards for her writing and speaking abilities.